The Ultimate "How-To" Guide To
PROTECT YOUR HEALTH, YOUR RIGHTS,
YOUR LIFE AND YOUR LOVED ONES
In Today's Era Of Modern Health Care

NSHORE √ PUBLISHING

Chicago, Illinois

150 S. Wacker Dr. Ste 2400, Chicago, IL 60606
www.northshoreRN.com

Patient Advocacy Matters © 2016 by NShore Publishing

An Imprint of Dreher Publishing in association with Quintessential Publishing Company, LLC

ISBN: 978-069279177-6

Library of Congress Control Number:

2016918959

Edited by Rhonda E. Alexander/Quintessential Publishing, LLC

Cover designed by Danijela Mijailovic

Manufactured and Printed in the United States of America

The Ultimate "How-To" Guide To
**PROTECT YOUR HEALTH, YOUR RIGHTS,
YOUR LIFE AND YOUR LOVED ONES**
In Today's Era Of Modern Health Care

by Teri Dreher, RN, CCRN, iRNPA
With Rhonda E. Alexander

NSHORE / PUBLISHING
Chicago, Illinois

Dedication

Dedicated to our family's Papa,
our loving and wise patriarch, counselor, supporter, and role
model in all matters of business and financial management.
You are the greatest curmudgeon of all and I love you
in spite of it; what would we do without you?

Thanks most of all for teaching me, a seasoned career
ICU nurse, how to advocate for my own family.
I never realized how powerful that role could be until
your critical illness off the coast of Belize in 2008.

Acknowledgements

This project has been a labor of love for me, as I genuinely want to help as many health care recipients as possible take charge of their health by becoming their own best advocate. If, somehow that is not possible, I pray they find someone who is armed with the knowledge I share in this book.

I am able to share the knowledge I gained in the pages in this book due to a lot of help from my team. I'd like to thank my editor, Rhonda Alexander most of all for her wisdom, guidance and encouragement throughout this entire project. Without her expertise and knowledge of how to turn my "beautiful mess" of stories into a book worth reading, nothing could have happened. She has been the "midwife" who helped me birth this book as no one else could have, since her passion for patient advocacy has been a personal mission. Years ago she made the difficult decision to step away from a promising career in corporate America to stay home with her own mother who sustained serious cognitive deficits after an anoxic brain injury. Caregivers understand as few others can, the power of advocating for your loved ones. We hope this book adds more tools in the tool belt for caregivers everywhere who struggle with heartbreaking family challenges.

My husband Dean, who is my best friend and supporter, believed in my talent and abilities for longer than anyone, and saw them firsthand when his father was in the midst of a medical crisis. His father Ed was the inspiration for my career change, and his wife Ramona has been my unwavering champion and supporter, and is probably telling all her bridge partners today to buy this book.

I'd like to thank my daughter Emma Dreher for her hours of typing, editing and encouraging me onward. To Dr. Patricia Schultz and my assistant Tracy Cook, I thank them also for believing in the power of advocacy and contributing to the whole project in so many ways.

I am enormously grateful to my former nurse manager Sharon Dmitrijevich who saw something more in me many years ago and encouraged me to pursue a career in patient advocacy. To Karen Mercereau of RN Patient Advocates, who wrote the foreward of this book, I will be forever grateful to her for actually equipping me to make a career out of my passion through her intensive and thorough training curriculum for nurse advocates in Arizona. She has been my champion and supporter since my career in advocacy began.

To my dear friends and colleagues Kate Curler, Jean Lyon and Danny McLane who contributed their own stories and wisdom to this book, I am forever in your debt.

You all helped me push through to ensure we finished this project with a bang. I am elated to have such a supportive community of friends, peers and associates who join me on this journey to true patient advocacy.

CONTENTS

Foreword

When I walk into an attorney's office to negotiate and try to read the contract, I become anxious because I do not speak "legalese." It is uncomfortable to participate in activities that will absolutely affect my life and I will not even comprehend what is happening and what I need to do. Mistakes happen all too often and they can cause me real harm.

Welcome to health care 101. Do you know your rights? Do you understand all the ramifications of your medications and treatment plan? Are you aware that the health insurance industry is dictating what can happen to you and what your physician must do in order to be reimbursed?

The stream of research and information in medicine today is at a high pitch and yet, do *you* understand that you really do have choices if only you could understand what they are? Do you realize that you absolutely can say, "No, not until I understand this better?"

The latest study on the number of misdiagnoses in the U.S. by the Institute of Medicine (2015) has demonstrated that there are 12 Million misdiagnoses each year. Why? Does this mean that our doctors and nurses have suddenly become substandard?

No.

A couple of factors create this perfect storm. First, the insurance industry dictates "production quotas" for health care providers so everyone is always in a very big hurry. Reimbursement is tied to levels of "production." That is a recipe for error and missed opportunities.

Secondly, many preventable medical errors occur due to a lack of accurate historical medical information; and unfortunately, it doesn't matter if the records are electronic or paper, they are usually not connected. An example of such an occurrence would be the scenario of a patient with a history of renal dysfunction who is experiencing severe pain. The patient arrives in the ER with a companion who is very upset and does not know what to tell the medical staff other than the history of the current issues. The patient is sent to have some radiology work done and a dye or "contrast" is administered in order to see more detail during the test. The patient's kidneys stop working properly due to the "contrast" chemicals. If only the physician had known about the patient's kidney history, there may have been a different outcome. Lack of contextual medical history leads to hundreds of thousands of preventable medical errors, some of them leading to death.

Dr. John T. James, a toxicologist at NASA, published the results of a national study in 2013 that investigated the number of preventable medical errors that contributed to a patient's death. Better sit down now.

Between 220,000 and 440,000 deaths due, at least in part, to preventable medical error occur every year! This was published in the Journal of Patient Safety in 2013. What if you do not know the proper questions to ask? By the way, this number is derived from only the hospitalized population, not the whole population.

Speaking of asking questions, it is surprising to note that the only major national groundbreaking study on health literacy was published by the Department of Health and Human Services. The National Assessment of Adult Literacy completed a study in 2003 that uncovered a startling fact: "Only 12 percent of U.S. adults had proficient health literacy. Over a third of U.S. adults—77 million people—would have difficulty with common health tasks, such as following directions on a prescription drug label..." Do YOU know the right questions to ask? These studies represent part of the context in which the field of patient advocacy has developed. Independent, RN-based patient advocacy, the most clinically in-depth form of patient advocacy, has delivered patient advocacy care across the U.S. since 2002.

Teri Dreher, RN, iRNPA (independent RN Patient Advocate) is one of the pioneers of this necessary and valuable service. The picture Ms. Dreher paints through the stories and facts in this eye-opening book is a picture all too familiar to millions of Americans. You will most likely see yourself or one of your loved ones reflected in the information presented here. Let Teri Dreher, RN, iRNPA, help you to understand how you can become an active participant (and advocate) in your own health care. The information in this book can help to save your life.

– Karen Mercereau, RN, iRNPA

Founder RN Patient Advocates, PLLC, 2002
Creator of the RN Patient Advocacy Process

Preface

Before I begin the story of the medical crisis that changed my life forever, I'd like to share a brief life history of my beloved father-in-law whom we lovingly refer to as "Papa," the man whose catastrophic health crisis catapulted me into the profession of health care advocacy. Papa loves his family dearly and has demonstrated that to all of us in countless ways over the years. I think I may actually have fallen in love with my in-laws before I did my husband. Papa is a very outgoing, likable guy who makes everyone feel welcome and liked. He was one of eight children who grew up in a poor farming community in Wisconsin. Since he was a child during the Great Depression, he experienced poverty firsthand. His father used to bring home "road kill" for dinner and he and his brothers from early on knew the value of hard physical labor. Papa grew up with lofty dreams of making it out of that little community and making something of himself. His childhood sweetheart, whom we call "Nanny," shared that dream, so they moved to the "big city" of Madison, Wisconsin. While in Madison, Papa attended night school while he worked two jobs to support his young family. He was a hard worker and eventually became the CFO at Baxter Health care in northern Illinois, and later leaving that job to start his own accouting firm in his hometown of Libertyville, Illinois. He was not just any accountant; he was tops in his field and a community leader. He enjoyed a lucrative career and invested wisely. All of his friends and clients respected him and agreed that his life was not too shabby for a small-town Wisconsin farm boy.

Education was a core family value to both Papa and Nanny, and once Papa received his accounting degree, he set the goal of one day paying for every one of his children to get the best education possible. Later in his career, Papa's generous and loving spirit, combined with his outstanding abilities as an accountant, allowed him to also provide every grandchild with higher education. We can never thank Papa enough for his love and sacrifice in providing for his family's education.

Papa is a wise man; he has taught all of us that there are no do-overs with family, and he has demonstrated through his actions the true meaning of loyalty to one's family. At the height of his career, his beloved Ramona was diagnosed with a particularly aggressive form of lung cancer. Upon learning of the diagnosis, Papa put the brakes on his career. His life priorities changed in a heartbeat and he dedicated the rest of his life to his family. He sold his accounting business and stayed by Ramona's side through an arduous course of extensive surgery, radiation, and chemotherapy that ultimately cured her disease. Even though it has left her with a partial right arm paralysis and chronic pain, we are so grateful that Ramona is considered cured of her cancer. We are grateful for them both and consider them both precious to our entire family.

Introduction

Patient advocacy is who I am and what I do. I am a voice for people without a voice, and I absolutely love using my decades of ICU experience to help save people's lives outside the hospital like I did for so many years within the boundaries of the ICU. Though my present career path is not nearly as lucrative as my former one, I must say, this is the greatest, best career decision of my life. The intangibles are priceless. Patient advocates make a difference every day, whether they are medically trained, or not. Today, everyone needs a patient advocate!

Some call it private professional health care advocacy, patient navigation or a variety of other names. The model I discuss here is the model of privately paid professionals who do not work for an institution or an insurance company. The lines of allegiance are clear when the patient pays for services. We do not work for the hospital; we do not work for the doctors, nor do we work for insurance companies. We are PRIVATE patient advocates, hired by patients and their families to protect patient rights and avoid medical error. We advocate for patients by–in extreme cases–helping to save their lives. As advocates for the patient, we also help patients to save money and most of all, we help save frustration for all who are struggling with modern health care.

Some of us have medical or nursing backgrounds, some are social workers, geriatric care managers and lay people who have studied the system well. We know how to come alongside patients and ensure they have better communication with health care providers. A big part of better communication with health care providers can be as simple as more education. More education, on the patient's part, empowers them as well, which helps protect them and improves their safety as they navigate through life's medical challenges along the way.

Modern health care is complex and frightening for many, and those who choose to hire their own advocate will almost always tell you, it is one of the best decisions they ever made. But consumers need to know that this is a fairly new field, only about ten years old, and there is no national accreditation process in place. Right now, that's the biggest challenge for leaders in this industry–to develop a test that will certify competency for both medical and nonmedical advocates. Not everyone needs a nurse or doctor to be his or her advocate. The level of medical complexity depends on the necessity of clinical expertise. Sometimes you simply need someone who is detail-oriented, organized and familiar with the protocol involved as it relates to your issue, if it is nonmedical.

To determine if a particular advocate is right for you, interview candidates carefully to make sure the advocate you choose has the right expertise and history of "wins" in similar situations. Personality, availability and business model of advocates vary widely and there should be a strong sense of correct "fit" with the advocate hired. The three national professional organizations, APHA, NAHAC and PPAI have resources on their websites to help people find an advocate in their area as well as guide them through the interview process. Just as every patient or client is unique, so are advocates.

To determine if you need an advocate, read as much as possible, don't be afraid to ask for referrals and do your due diligence to become informed about this new and growing field. This new field is expanding quickly, and will grow to meet the growing needs of our society. In a perfect world, no one *should* need his or her own advocate. However, the changes occurring in the current health care system mean most nurses and doctors from inside the system will tell you that no one has the time to spend talking with patients as much as they would like, and as much as they used to do.

Patient advocates fill gaps that need to be filled to make certain the patient remains number one at all times. Patient advocates are part of the village we all need to raise a child; and to save, maintain and even improve the quality of a life. May all my readers help us pass the word: patient advocates are here to stay because all is fair in love and patient advocacy!

Section I
The Beginning
of This Journey

How did this all come about? How did I go from being a dedicated ICU nurse for over 30 years to taking this leap of faith to become an advocate for the sick, the disabled and my favorite group, the seniors?

In this section, I share my definition of modern health care as it relates to the world we are living in today as well as a couple of stories that compelled me to take action–action that changed the trajectory of my career, my life and I hope, the lives of those who need a village of protection to help ensure their safety and their health.

By the time you finish this chapter, you'll have a true sense of what it means to advocate for someone. You will also see, through the experiences I share, how challenging situations can escalate to a point of no return; and unfortunately how, all too often, if only there were an advocate for the patient in place, the outcome would have been better for everyone involved.

You will also find the "Tips to Equip" within, or at the end of each chapter. These tips are pulled directly from sections within the chapter to equip you with information that can help you advocate for your loved ones, or on your own behalf, depending on the situation. These are also tips to educate you, so you have a better sense of what "right" and when something doesn't feel right. Finally, these tips are also in place to help you as you decide whether a patient advocate is the right fit to step in and help you move through a particularly challenging period of your quest for the best health care.

Chapter 1

Modern Health Care
And My Inspiration For Advocacy

My Inspiration for Patient Advocacy

Over the years, I've seen a lot of people die—I have worked in ICU and oncology units in some of the best hospitals throughout the country over the past thirty-something years. I'll tell you something: no one ever wishes they had worked harder or made more money on their deathbed. Though it is true that men want to know that their families are well provided for, wealth is not as important as you think it might be when you are dying. The only thing that matters is whom you love and who loves you. If you hold material possessions side-by-side with your investments of love and support for your family, family wins every time. Period. We get one chance to make a difference in the world, and family is a pretty good return on investment for the vast majority of people I know. I've learned this by watching hundreds of people die over the years. It makes me more intentional about the legacy I am passing on to my own children. I hope they remember me as a person who placed people, and particularly family, as much more valuable than money. Always. Even when we do not realize it, our families watch every decision we make, and I pray that I pass that value along.

I was excited about going on my first cruise to Belize at the age of 52. I had heard from many of my friends that a cruise was a wonderful way to relax on vacation. To celebrate their 50th wedding anniversary, my in-laws decided to take their entire family on a cruise. They had wisely realized that they had all the "stuff" they needed; their gift to themselves would be some uninterrupted quality time with all of their children, their spouses, and grandchildren! To me, it was a dream come true—a seven-day excursion to the Caribbean Islands with unlimited food, endless entertainment, sun and poolside lounge chairs where I could kick back with my entire family. An entire week's reprieve from my career as an Intensive Care Unit nurse, freedom from housecleaning and all the other day-to-day duties! The grandchildren could take advantage of dozens of options for a good time while the rest of us could lounge around the pool, sipping margaritas, reading long-neglected books and taking naps whenever we felt like it. What fun we would have, all fourteen of us vacationing together! But my dream vacation turned into a medical crisis, and a patient advocate was born.

So what happened in Belize that changed the course of our family's history and my own professional life forever? We had a catastrophic medical emergency while we were on that cruise ship, docked off the shore of Belize. My father-in-law developed a blood clot the size of Rhode Island in his vena cava, the largest vein in the human body. The blood clot was lodged between his heart and his ankles, stopping blood flow to his organs, threatening to kill him at any moment. He should have gone from his stateroom directly to an intensive care unit, but there was no ICU on board that cruise ship, and no ICU where we were docked in Belize, either. Good thing he had the next best thing on board: an ICU nurse in the family.

Looking back, I can see that we should have paid closer attention when leaving for the airport two days earlier. Papa had complained of some minor low back and hip pain, which he attributed to falling asleep in an awkward position while we were getting into the limo. We have always viewed Papa as a pretty healthy 76-year-old man, though I knew he had a hereditary disorder where his blood clots too easily. A couple of months earlier, he had experienced a fainting spell and was found to have a couple of blood clots in his lungs. Blood clots in the lungs, known as pulmonary emboli, begin in the legs and dislodge and travel northbound via the inferior vena cava and become lodged in the pulmonary artery where they are often fatal. Before our cruise, surgeons had placed a special "filter" in his vena cava (the same vein that developed the huge clot on the cruise) to prevent blood clots in his legs from reaching his lungs. This filter made us feel confident that he would not develop any serious blood clots to his lungs.

So when Papa fainted outside the dining room two days into our cruise, we all thought it was odd, but we were not alarmed. After all, he had the filter, so we felt very confident that it was not a blood clot. We had him checked out by the ship's doctor (a lovely South African gentleman whom I will never forget) and the plan was to have him come back for another clinic visit the next morning to make certain all was well, just to be on the safe side. We were satisfied and appreciative of the physician's concern and thorough examination.

The next morning when I arrived at Nanny and Papa's stateroom to accompany him back to the ship's medical clinic, I got quite a shock. Lying in bed was my beloved father-in-law, cold and clammy, with both legs swollen and starting to turn a nasty shade of blue (what we in the medical world call cyanosis, caused by lack of oxygen flow). Nanny said, "He's having a hard time getting to the bathroom."

I think my initial thoughts went something like, "Holy Mother of God, we are in deep trouble now."

Not wanting to cause undue alarm in a situation I knew was about to become a serious medical situation, I calmly asked a few questions and wanted to get Papa settled into a wheelchair so we could take him to see the ship's physician as quickly as possible. Nanny knew something was not quite right, but she did not know how sick he was and I was not about to tell her right then and risk having her get hysterical on me. Then I would have two problems to deal with.

While I was getting Papa into the wheelchair, I noticed things that others would only glance at. I was in full ICU-nurse-crisis-mode and remarkably calm, confident, and hyper-alert. If you ever see ICU nurses become very calm, with a concerned look on their face, you might be in deep trouble. I knew in an instant, from years of honing my ICU assessment skills and my expertise as a cardiovascular nurse clinician, that my father-in-law had just clotted off his IVC filter, effectively halting blood flow to his lungs from his body below the diaphragm. Body organs need blood flow. This was a serious issue. The lack of blood flow from his legs to his upper body was causing his legs to swell and severely impairing his circulation. The cold, clammy skin told me he was going into shock. I knew that low blood flow to his kidneys and bowel could cause serious complications if we did not restore it quickly. I noticed all of these things and thought about their ramifications while calmly wheeling him down the hallway to the ship's physician. I formulated in my mind what medical professionals would call a differential diagnosis and plan of care, based on my findings. I hoped I was wrong.

I watched the ship's doctor examine Papa and grew more alarmed as I noticed that he also had that same very calm, very quiet and concerned expression on his face. I was sure I had that look plastered on my own face the previous thirty minutes. I asked him out into the hall and discussed my suspicions.

"I think he's clotted off his IVC filter. What do you think?" I ventured.

"Yep, looks like we may have a serious problem here," the doctor replied.

Unfortunately, there was no ultrasound machine on the ship. The closest ultrasound machine was at a community hospital in Belize. Being a third world country, we knew it would not be a major university hospital but we decided to take him off the ship and transfer him there where they could do a further diagnostic workup and proceed from there. At least, I reasoned, they would surely have intravenous blood thinners (like Heparin) that would prevent the clot from progressing and hopefully Papa's own body would slowly be able to break down the clot that was growing by the minute. Having been in developing countries' medical centers many times before while traveling to Africa on medical mission trips, I was curious about what we would actually find in Belize. I wondered if this hospital would be able to handle a full-blown medical emergency if, God forbid, Papa's heart or breathing stopped.

While all of this went on in my mind's eye, Papa was laughing and joking, charming the ship's nurse and medical technician, oblivious to what was about to happen. After I conveyed my suspicions to the family, they all decided that I would be the logical choice to go with him as he left the ship that day, and we all agreed to stay in close contact by cell phone. Nanny started to cry as she kissed him good-bye while everyone else stood around reassuring themselves that it would all be fine and we would reunite in a day or two (as for me, I wasn't so sure, but I stayed quiet and smiled calmly. There was no sense in taking the entire family off the ship, as there was nothing any of them could do, and truthfully, paying attention to everyone's opinions would only distract me from the work involved in keeping a close eye on Papa. As we left the ship that day I prayed hard while staying calm and reassuring, but I was also hyper-alert for every detail, every symptom, that could herald the onset of an acute medical emergency (or "adverse medical outcome" as they say in hospital lingo).

We got to the hospital in Belize that day and the very tiny emergency room looked to be a slight improvement over the African hospitals I've seen before, so I felt fairly confident that they should be able to help. Treatment of choice would likely initially be Heparin through an IV to prevent further blood clots from forming, and to wait seven to 10 days for the body's normal clot/fibrin breakdown process to dissolve the blood clot. If this had been a major medical center, Papa would've been taken immediately to the interventional radiology department and had the clot manually extracted by a specially trained physician; we did not have that option in Belize. The trouble was that we had no way of knowing how extensive the blood clot was. An antiquated ultrasound machine was able to determine that Papa had blood clots in both of his legs, but it malfunctioned and broke down halfway through the test. The doctor's best guess was that the clots were fairly extensive, so we decided that we would admit Papa to the hospital and stay on a Heparin drip for a few days and see what happened.

For three days we stayed in the small hospital room together—I in one bed, Papa in another. He remained on bed rest with a continual infusion of Heparin to prevent further clot formation. Heparin does not actually dissolve clots; a stronger category of medicine known as thrombolytics will dissolve clots, but they are high-risk medications only given under very limited circumstances. Papa would not have qualified for those anyway due to previous medical problems related to his hereditary blood-clotting disorder. This was not an ideal treatment, but it was the best we had. I felt as though we were still sitting on a ticking time bomb, hoping for the best.

The third day in the hospital was Thanksgiving, and the kind hospital chef who cooked, served, and cleared the food for every patient in the facility tried hard to make our day pleasant. She did her best with a Belizean version of a Thanksgiving dinner. She was sweet and the dinner was lovely, though we missed our family very much. Everyone at the hospital was very nice: the doctor, nurses, cleaning staff and the chef who brought us that special meal. We were grateful for all of them on that Thanksgiving Day. Little did I realize that it was the calm before the storm, and I was about to have my nursing instincts and every skill I'd learned during the course of my career tested to the very limits of my capacity.

Dr. O came into the room with some special news that day which he was certain would please us: Papa would now be allowed to get out of bed and walk to the bathroom. Papa was delighted: me, not so much. Small warning bells went off in my head and I questioned him (very politely, of course; it's always a good idea to be respectful and polite to one's health care providers).

"Are you sure?" I asked the doctor.

He assured me that Papa was fine and it was time to progressively increase his activity in anticipation of a quick discharge. He related his concern that older people who stay in bed too long get weaker and weaker, which I knew to be true from experience.

I went along with the plan after he left and helped Papa walk to the bathroom. Besides feeling a little dizzy, he was walking well and he looked forward to some alone time in the bathroom, away from the watchful eyes of his daughter-in-law.

As I stood outside the bathroom door that day, I struggled with two conflicting priorities. First, I wanted to guard my father-in-law's health and safety, but regretfully I also wanted to be seen by the medical staff as a source of help rather than a hindrance to his care. Nurses and doctors are used to seeing family members behaving badly in a health care crisis, and I did not want to be seen as a "problem" family member that they needed to tiptoe around. I'm a good nurse, but also a nice person, so I did not want to offend the doctor. I went along with his plan even though it made me uneasy. I knew the clot had not dissolved yet, from my knowledge of the pathophysiology of the hematological system (blood disorders, such as anemia, leukemia, clotting disorders).

After about three minutes in the bathroom, I called out to Papa: "Are you okay in there?" I got no answer. I knocked on the door and heard him mumble, "I don't feel so good…"

I opened the door and my jaw dropped: standing before me was my father-in-law, quickly turning the darkest shade of purple I had ever seen anyone turn and still be alive. He was dying right before my eyes. So I quickly did what any seasoned ICU nurse would do: I put my emotions up on a shelf and initiated the emergency response system, calling a code blue.

As I called for help and half-carried Papa back to bed, lifting his feet up higher than his head on to pillows, I soon breathed a sigh of relief as the blood started returning to his face and he became more alert. The blood flow to his brain and heart had been severely impaired due to the extensive clot that was acting like a beaver's dam in his vena cava, the main river of the circulatory system. Everything downstream of his clotted-off IVC filter was backing up, and his body could not break down the clot quickly enough. I saw that he could not stand up for more than a minute or two without becoming symptomatic, so I knew the clot was going to need more aggressive intervention than the Heparin drip he had been receiving. All this I knew from my past clinical experience and finely-honed assessment skills from decades of ICU bedside nursing. Book knowledge is one thing, but clinical savvy is worth its weight in gold when dealing with acute medical emergencies. Doctors and nurses have told me for years how glad they are when I am running the code in hospitals. They value clinical experience as well, and they know how important it is to stay calm and collected as you multi-task in the midst of a code situation.

It was, however, a completely new challenge to try to save the life of a family member. Our beloved patriarch's life was literally in my hands now, and it scared me to death. After making certain he was stabilizing, I excused myself to the bathroom for a few minutes and had a good cry before launching into the next leg of our journey. I came out of the bathroom with firm resolve to move quickly so that I could get him back to the U.S.; he could get appropriate emergency treatment quickly there.

All of this ran through my mind as the entire medical and nursing staff gathered around Papa's bed in the Belizean hospital that day, the doctor looking sheepishly down at his shoes, a nervous tic appearing around his left temple. I took a deep breath after Papa's blood pressure slowly return to normal, and he became more alert, I wondered what happened.

I turned to the doctor, who minutes earlier had assured me that his patient would be "just fine" to get out of bed that day, and said simply, "We're going back to the U.S. today."

The next few hours were a blur of phone calls, requesting copies of tests and X-rays and speaking with the travel insurance carrier that my in-laws had wisely contracted prior to the trip.

It would take too long to get a special MED-EVAC plane into this tiny Caribbean community, so we compromised for the sake of expediency. The first plane leaving for Miami would depart in three hours, so the agent booked two first-class seats and I instructed the attendants that he would not be allowed to stand up for any reason. He would fly with his head reclined and feet up all the way back home to Chicago, going through customs in Miami with an escort and an ICU nurse at his side.

The trip back to Chicago was stressful for me, but hey—I'm a nurse and I thrive on excitement. Put me in a classroom with twenty-five children for an hour and I will have a nervous breakdown, but put me in an ICU with the sickest patient they have, and I am in my element. I love saving people's lives for a living. Holistic nursing—providing physical, emotional, and spiritual support to people in great need, is what I do best. It is extremely rewarding and has made me a better human being. I am proud to be a nurse. It's one of the noblest professions there is.

As I sat next to Papa that day on the plane and stayed by his side as we made our way back to the U.S., I played my role well—alert but not alarmist. I knew deep down that Papa could die at any moment; the change in cabin pressure could trigger a sudden catastrophic event, but I felt we had no choice but to try. People who are not physically healthy should not fly. If they are really unhealthy, they may not even be stable enough to travel several hours home by ambulance. I've had patients who begged to go home on hospice when their cancer grew worse in spite of treatment, and they died on the way home. That's tough for families to live with.

Once we arrived at O'Hare and settled into a limousine headed for our community's largest hospital, we were both breathing a little easier. Finally, our ordeal would be over soon. Our safe haven was in sight.

We arrived at the hospital ER at about 1:00 a.m. and explained to the triage nurse at the front desk that Papa was in the midst of a medical emergency. Unfortunately, dear Papa became a charming businessman again, which works pretty well when negotiating business deals. He turned on the charm and chatted amiably with the ER nurse, looking for all the world as if he were still on vacation. As he sat in the wheelchair with no complaints whatsoever, he really did not look sick. The triage nurse probably relayed that impression to the physician as well. After a few minutes of pleasant conversation, we were ushered into an ER bay and I helped him get onto the cart and put on a hospital gown. A few moments passed and Dr. "C" walked in. We relayed the events of the past four days and he listened politely, making a few notes on Papa's paper chart. After a few more questions and polite nods of the head, the doctor excused himself to call my father-in-law's primary care physician. I was certain that Papa would soon be admitted and scheduled for an early interventional radiology procedure the next morning.

Now, to be fair to the ER doctor, I never tell people I am an ICU nurse when I show up with family members to the ER. I want to see how the lay person (nonmedical people) are treated. I think everyone should be treated equally in a hospital, and I don't want anyone assuming anything about me either just because I'm an ICU nurse. My feeling is that if a hospital treats all patients with respect, kindness, and highly competent care in an ER, then the hospital probably has a culture of premium quality care.

So when Dr. C came back to deliver his diagnosis and plan of care, I was all ears.

He said, "So I called Dr. M and told him what's going on with you, and Dr. M said that these things happen sometimes, and you can go home on subcutaneous Lovenox (a form of blood thinner less potent than the Heparin drip he had been on in Belize) and you should be fine."

You can probably imagine the long silence from me.

After collecting myself for a few seconds, I could hold it in no longer. I crossed my arms, looked into the doctor's eyes, and said firmly, "That is not going to happen. We just told you all the reasons why I believe my father-in-law has clotted off his IVC filter. He cannot even stand up without passing out. He has a blood clot that is turning into concrete from his diaphragm all the way down both legs. Look at his feet! We are not going anywhere until he goes to the interventional lab in a few hours and they inject dye into his vena cava that proves I am wrong. You go call Dr. T [my cardiologist friend] and tell him that Teri Dreher is in the ER with her father-in-law and she is being 'difficult.' He'll know what to do. We are not going anywhere, sir."

The good doctor had probably started to realize by now that I was in the medical field. He politely excused himself to call Dr. T. Within three minutes, he returned and shared that Dr. T wanted my father-in-law admitted and scheduled for a venogram at 8:00 a.m.

Teri Dreher

Papa had never seen me get riled up before, so in the days to come, he relayed to all his friends how Teri had assertively interacted with the ER physician. Ever since then, whenever the story comes up again, I always tell my family to remember that nice doctors are not always right. Just because they stride confidently into your room and tell you what *should* happen does not mean you need to go along with their plan. It's a joint decision. ER doctors have about five minutes to spend with each patient and thirty minutes to spend with their chart. They don't have time to hear every minute detail of your past medical history. Be polite, be respectful of their time, but remember that you know your family member better than anyone, so trust your instincts and question the plan if it doesn't feel right.

The next morning when I arrived at 7:30 a.m., Papa was already in the interventional radiology lab. An interventional radiology lab is similar to a heart catheterization lab (where heart attacks are treated). They are run by interventional radiologists—physicians who are experts at reading x-rays, CT scans, and MRI's, but have also had additional extensive training in a wide variety of minimally invasive vascular procedures that routinely save people's lives. Think of an interventional radiologist as a cream-of-the-crop radiologist with a surgeon's personality. They are the gods of the radiology world! The physician emerged from the room four and a half hours later, telling us he had never seen such an extensive thrombus (blood clot). He used a microscopic type of high-tech drill and employed multiple attempts to free the clot and open up his circulation once more, restoring blood flow to his legs and vital organs. What a relief!

26

Patient Advocacy Matters

After his procedure in the interventional radiology lab, Papa went to the ICU that day for recovery and, once again, we optimistically assumed that he would quickly recover and we would all be on our way out the door soon. It was not to be. My dear father-in-law endured every complication known to man, and our family witnessed firsthand the best and worst of medical care over the ensuing two months. After the first few near-death experiences, my friend Dr. T contacted a colleague at Rush Presbyterian St. Luke's Hospital in Chicago who happened to be one of the world's top experts in rare congenital clotting disorders. These doctors, Dr. T and Dr. V, saved my father-in-law's life. Rush's team of expert interventional radiologists performed multiple life-saving procedures. Dr. "L" eventually performed a procedure on him that stopped persistent bleeding, though it had only been done experimentally twice before. I am grateful for these men. They are heroes and our family will be forever grateful to every one of them.

During these six weeks of Papa's hospitalizations in Belize and Illinois, I had a chance to view the hospital experience from the inside out, as a family member. This completely foreign vantage point was, for me, a very valuable learning experience—an epiphany of sorts. Communication problems between practitioners, multiple crises requiring emergent surgical procedures, allergic reactions to medicines, almost bleeding to death, descending into hemorrhagic shock, and several ICU admissions convinced me of the great need for professional advocacy.

What would have happened if I had not been with our beloved patriarch when disaster struck? The entire family affirmed that they knew he would have died if I had not been there. I was just doing

27

my job and thinking of little else but standing guard, watching and observing, asking all the right questions, and asserting myself if I felt he was not receiving the best care. I knew my father-in-law better than any of the care providers did, plus I had the advantage of advanced clinical expertise. Not many families have that luxury. Fortunately, my father-in-law is healthier today than he was in 2008 and we had a positive outcome. Sadly, not everyone is so fortunate.

When I returned to work after our family's six-week ordeal, I had new eyes and new empathy to truly understand what families are going through, and I began to advocate even more strongly for patient safety. Many years earlier, I had come close to being fired over advocating for a patient who was having multiple complications from a major surgery. When I asked the doctor why my patient was not being sent for scans and exploratory surgery for multiple episodes of bleeding, I soon found myself on a ten-day suspension from work for a charting omission.

To clarify, I'm sure my suspension had nothing to do with the charting omission error; those omissions happen all the time. Though I was still satisfied in my heart that I had made the right decision to stand up for the patient and question the surgeon's judgment, I heard the message loud and clear: nurses who stand up against powerful, money-making surgeons, and threaten the image of the hospital by drawing attention to errors, can quickly find themselves labeled "expendable." Nurses have a bill of rights just as patients do, and one of our rights states that we should not be persecuted for advocating for patients, but the facts can be twisted any way facilities want them to—and who wants to fight big business?

Many nurses are playing it safe these days, keeping their heads down and not making waves unless they have to. We are the ambassadors for the hospitals and we are to provide quality care, avoid errors, and make the hospital look good. This is a tall order, considering the time constraints that our computers demand. Nursing is a tough profession, taking a toll on our minds, hearts, and backs. A looming shortage of nurses and primary care physicians is predicted to peak in 2018. It will be interesting to watch how the hospital industry endeavors to fill the gaps—as well as how the shortages will affect patient care. Something's gotta give.

What is Modern Health Care?

What Modern Health care Means to Me (as a nurse)

I tread lightly here as I share some of my impressions of what modern health care means to me as a nurse. I have seen it from the inside as an ICU nurse and from the outside, as I know what many of you are going through if you have had frustrations with modern health care. I have seen the fear, outrage and shock as our family went through our own medical calamity, and I realize it's not an isolated incident. I've also seen modern health care, in its current incarnation, from years of studying the Affordable Care Act. From my point of view, modern health care falls under two very large umbrellas: The quality of health care and the financial ramifications stemming from the inception of the Affordable Care Act.

There are no villains in the world of modern health care, but the U.S. health care system is fractured in many ways and it's not always safe going into the hospital for a multitude of reasons. I think it's safe to say it will be quite awhile before America has her health care "mess" straightened out because, in its prior state, the U.S. health care system was not sustainable with costs running away as they were before March 2010, which is when President Obama signed the law into being.

From a financial standpoint, there is little "affordable" about the Affordable Care Act. Health care costs are still rising, albeit at a somewhat slower pace. The costs of insurance have risen at least 40 percent for those paying for private insurance, and deductibles have never been higher. Out of pocket medical expenses are higher than ever and everyone is frustrated. Insurance brokers are going out of business at record rates since commissions have been eliminated, and the insurance landscape is changing daily.

The Affordable Care Act, or "Obama Care," as it is often referred, is the most radical change within the health care system to which modern health care refers. Whether you are a liberal, or conservative, there are many vantage points that are valid when looking at the ACA from different perspectives. There are many wonderful provisions of the ACA: closing of the donut hole for Medicare recipients, making drug costs more affordable, free prevention screenings for cancer, yearly free physicals (as long as no treatment or problems are addressed), ambulatory services, emergency care, maternity and mental health services, etc. The benefits to the Medicaid population cannot be overstated; and general access to health care for the poor has improved, especially in urban areas. Detractors still say that it places undue restrictions on physicians to deliver care they know their patients need. Doctors can no longer just think about the patient; they must think about insurance limitations, costs, ICD-9 codes (used to code patient's diagnosis for insurance companies to pay claims for services rendered) and charting correctly, which takes time.

According to the Examiner.com website, New Jersey family physician, Dr. John Tedeschi said, "Just as a guitar string has to be tuned, so does a person's health to get the right tone. The government has taken away, or refocused the intelligence part of the tuning, and has just about destroyed the creative, or compassion component. Now, with "Obama Care," we are left with an incompetent mechanism that does not have the best interests of the patient in mind." Another physician friend of mine, who prefers not to be quoted, describes deep discouragement at working so hard to build up a successful cardiology practice, only to have to spend over $25,000 on new computers that would comply with government regulations for electronic health record charting. At the same time, his practice had to stop doing stress tests in the office with the new, modern equipment they had just bought because reimbursement rates favored hospital-based stress tests after Obama Care came into being. Many doctors are struggling to keep their practice focused on patient care, but due to the sheer amount of documentation required for insurance accounting purposes, doctors feel their attention is diverted away from patient care in favor of computer work. Many are retiring very discouraged and worried about how their aging patients will fare in this brand, new world of health care.

Not all doctors are so negative towards post Affordable Care Act medicine. In large part, doctors are split along political party lines, with 87 percent of physicians who lean towards the Democratic Party reporting that they feel, "mostly positive" about the impact of Obama Care. In contrast, the exact same number of Republicans felt it had a negative impact on quality, safety and cost. Independents tended to lean toward a more negative opinion, according to a study published by Kaiser Health in 2015.

Though most will agree that the ACA has negatively impacted patients financially, if questioned, they realize that the state of American health care could not continue without drastic change. The U.S. has the most expensive health care system in the world and it is far from the highest quality.

The World Health Organization rates the quality of the U.S. health system somewhere between #25 and #27 in terms of quality, safety and cost. A study published by the Wall Street Journal in June of 2016 showed that medical error is STILL the third leading cause of death in America today. Why is it so dangerous to be a patient in hospitals today in America? A comprehensive overview can be found in the landmark study from 1999 called, "To Err is Human: Building a Better Health care System," which claimed that about 30 percent of patients who enter a hospital will incur some sort of "adverse medical outcome," which is code for medical error. It can be something as simple as an allergic reaction to a new medication, to something as extreme as a wrong body part being removed, or sponges left inside the body during surgery that leads to sepsis (a blood infection) and even death.

The quality of health care has declined, the numbers of medical errors are on the rise, as excellent physicians and nurses leave their professions in large numbers. This does not bode well for health care in the United States.

The statistics are there to back up what we have observed: many physicians have left private practice or are thinking of leaving medicine due to the heavy demands placed upon them. (Jauhar, 2014) Physicians are disheartened with medicine. In a survey of 12,000 physicians, only six percent said their morale was positive. (Jauhar, 2014) The truth is, we all need physicians, and we don't want to see them leaving their profession.

Why are physicians leaving practice? In a Wall Street Journal article entitled, "Why Doctors Are Sick Of Their Profession" (Jauhar, 2014), Dr. Sandeep Jauhar reminisces how physicians in the mid-twentieth century were "the pillars of any community," and becoming a physician was a most noble profession. Doctors were free to set their own hours and their own fees, and practiced medicine without answering to administrative restrictions. As medicine began to become more "managed" with the development of HMO's in the 1970's, physician autonomy in making medical decisions decreased, as did physician compensation. This has only worsened with the Affordable Care Act where reimbursement has decreased further and administrative entanglements tie doctors up from seeing patients.

Today's physicians are financially struggling. Many people assume that physicians are all wealthy. These days, physician income is lower due to increased expenses in operating a medical practice (particularly medical malpractice insurance premiums) combined with lower reimbursement rates from insurance companies. Studies cite that physicians are now making less money per year than 20 years ago while seeing twice as many patients per day. (Jauhar, 2014)

With medical malpractice suits at an all time high, physicians are paying exorbitant premiums for their malpractice insurance. One fine physician had such a high malpractice insurance premium that he remarked, "The day that my malpractice exceeds my income, I'm outta here!" Sadly, many excellent physicians share his sentiments.

Then there's the issue of low reimbursement rates by private insurance carriers and Medicare. A physician may bill, for example, $1800 for perform a colon cancer screening known as a colonoscopy, and only be paid $200 by the patient's insurance company. The low insurance reimbursement puts physicians under pressure to work faster and see more patients in a day in order to make ends meet.

In order to increase the number of patients seen in a day (and thus increase office revenue), some doctors have resorted to hiring "physician assistants" (PAs); this is not ideal either as it brings the other component of the modern health care umbrella into play: quality health care. Something that might surprise you is how little training a PA has compared to a physician. Your physician must first earn an undergraduate degree, then attend four years of medical school (two years spent "in the books" and two years spent in the hospitals experiencing hands-on learning in how to treat patients). After those four years, you are then called doctor. Physicians then spend a year in an "internship" and during that year, they are applying for a residency position. Residency can last anywhere from three to seven years depending upon the medical specialty they have chosen.

In contrast, a PA's training consists of completing an undergraduate college degree and then only two years obtaining a master's degree in Physician Assistant Practice before they are off examining, diagnosing, and treating patients. In summary, PAs spend a total of two years combined on the textbook studies and the clinical practice to become a PA and start working with actual human beings. How can this be? PAs are "physician assistants," but the physician who employs the PA is liable for their work as well as their own.

It used to be that the physician had to be present in the office while the PA was seeing patients, and their charts had to be countersigned by the physician, but that has changed too. Over

29 states have passed legislation that allows PAs to see patients without countersignature by a physician. (Japsen, 2016).

In our era of everyone suing everyone, physicians live with a constant worry of being sued, or "missing something," yet their hands are tied by insurance company policies that require "preapproval" (which sometimes result in non-approval of coverage) for important tests like CT scans, MRI's and the like. Want to have some blood work done? The physician had better come up with legitimate diagnoses that "justify" the blood tests, or they won't be paid for. This certainly contributes to low morale.

Electronic health record systems are a constant thorn in physicians' sides. Where once the patient was the focus of care and doctors could spend the time necessary to listen to their patients, thoroughly examine them, and carefully think through treatment plans, now the computer takes center stage. One doctor described the hospital's "documentation specialists," hospital employees whose job it is to make sure that the physician documentation will yield the best payment from the insurance company, as a constant source of harassment to doctors. He spoke of floods of emails reminding him of some omission in the unwieldy computer charting system. These types of emails are unpleasant distractions and aggravations in the lives of talented and caring physicians; they'd rather focus on the patients than on the computer! Hospitals' medical record departments routinely send doctors threatening letters telling them that their hospital privileges will be removed if they do not get caught up with their charting, and it's getting harder and harder to get caught up these days.

It's no wonder that many excellent primary care physicians are giving in to the pressure to allow physicians known as "hospitalists" to manage their patients when they go into the hospital. A hospitalist is a physician, usually an internal medicine specialist, employed by the hospital to care for hospitalized patients. That means the patient's private physician won't even come and see them while they're in the hospital. Most patients, especially seniors, would much rather have their personal physicians manage their care when they are hospitalized. One woman told the story of how she saw three different hospitalists and two specialists when she was in the hospital. She was so confused—she had no idea who was handling what!

Our broken system and burned-out physicians are compromising what used to be excellent care. Physicians used to be willing to take care of patients without financial resources– it was just "the right thing to do." Physicians are stretched so far today that this is occurring less and less.

There is a shortage of primary care physicians, and it's expected to get much worse. Many primary care physicians have now reached baby boomer age and are retiring, and primary care is not an area that many new graduates want to get into because of low reimbursement and long hours.

Registered nurses are leaving their profession as well. When I started my health consultancy business, North Shore Patient Advocates (now NShore Patient Advocates), in the fall of 2011, it was largely a result of my father-in-law's health crisis in the hospitals in Belize and Illinois. I saw the cracks in our increasingly complex U.S. health care system from a family member's perspective. At the time, I was an ICU nurse with 38 years of strong clinical experience. I had also worked as a cardiovascular nurse clinician for a busy interventional cardiologist. I was comfortable with handling complex medical and surgical patients with multi-system pathology. I loved the pace of the intensive care unit and had always been a natural patient advocate, speaking up for patients and families, offering physical, emotional, and spiritual support to those in crisis. And I still loved the art and practice of bedside nursing. But I had never experienced firsthand the terror and frustration that families experience when a loved one has a medical crisis.

As you have probably realized by now, I loved working as an ICU nurse. But nursing has changed from how I was trained in nursing school, and how I practiced for most of my career. As one of their many excellent qualities, nurses have been taught to utilize keen powers of observation and to critically analyze tests and clinical findings.

Sadly, the time that we used to spend doing that is now being severely reduced by excessive computerized medical record keeping requirements needed to protect the hospital's liability. The new mantra is, "If it did not get charted, it did not happen." Whereas it used to take 20-30 minutes per day to chart by hand, we now have to spend two to three hours per patient, per day feeding the computer monster. I cannot count how many times I have spent over an hour charting a morning assessment, only to run to attend to an emergent patient need without saving my data and poof! All of that data is gone and I must start the entire process over again. I soon saw the promises of computers making our job easier as a myth; nothing was easy any longer and scores of nurses have are leaving the profession over the computerized records. Why not simply return to paper charts? It is a federal mandate that we must have electronic records!

Nurses now attend seminars solely dedicated to how to "cover our behinds" above all else. This is frustrating for genuinely caring individuals who have a passion to help and heal people rather than focusing most of our attention on computers. Most personal care in hospitals is now provided by certified nursing assistants (CNAs). CNAs complete a certificate program, typically at a junior college, so naturally they don't have the same level of powers of observation and analysis as registered nurses. Don't get me wrong, though, we nurses are grateful to have them help us. Nurses are drowning in technology and we all miss our patients; CNAs are to nurses what nurse practitioners and physician assistants are to doctors. We all need help doing our jobs.

In his Wall St. Journal article, Dr. Jauhar made an astute statement when he said, "Unhappy doctors make for unhappy patients." (Jauhar, 2014) He remarked, "For many of us, it is rare to find a primary physician who can remember us from visit to visit, let alone come to know us in depth or with any meaning or relevancy." (Jauhar, 2014) This really drives home the point that unhappy physicians make for unhappy patients.

This true story illustrates how an unhappy physician creates unhappy patients. Not long ago, a woman came to us with a plea to help her son. He had previously been admitted to a hospital with a kidney stone that was causing severe pain. The urologist had placed a stent into the man's kidney and bladder to allow the stone to pass. Since the stent was so uncomfortable, the young man had been unable to return to his job as a laborer. And since he had no insurance, he applied for Medicaid at the hospital, but was told it would be several weeks or months before he would be approved.

When it was time to have the stent removed, the young man called the surgeon's office to set up the appointment for the removal but was told that, unless he could come up with $1,000 cash, he would not be seen and the stent would not be removed. The patient had submitted proof that he was doing all that he could to get covered by Medicaid. Unfortunately, Medicaid now reimburses physicians at such low rates that many practitioners refuse to accept Medicaid patients.

The paradox was that this unfortunate young man, unable to work due to the pain from the stent, yet not able to have it removed without cash in hand, would have been forced to go to an emergency room and accrue another large hospital bill for pain control and to force someone's hand to remove the stent. These are some of the harsh realities facing modern health care: there are still people falling through the cracks.

My heart broke for this young man. Even though he could not afford a private advocate, we decided to take his case on a pro-bono basis. It was simply unethical to allow this patient to stay in pain because he had no money. Someone needed to stand up and help, regardless of his financial status. Fortunately, this story has a happy ending: when we intervened as this young man's private patient advocate, the surgeon's office was very accommodating in scheduling the stent removal. The young man was happy to have his story shared in hopes of educating and inspiring others. As health care professionals, we all take an oath to follow a code of ethics, and ethically there are times and circumstances where each of us has to stand up and do the right thing without regard for financial compensation.

This new world of health care is very much about money, marketing and efficiency. In a lot of ways, we are in "quite a pickle" as my grandmother would say. My concern for patients today is for their safety. Modern health care is becoming increasingly fragmented, which can easily lead to dangerous gaps in communication. The patient needs to remain at the center of the model of care. Doctors, nurses, and patients know that our present health care system is seriously flawed. Something has got to change before more patients get hurt, and before more fine physicians hang up their stethoscopes and leave.

While it is almost impossible for health care professionals to keep up with the changes, never mind the consumer, I do see signs of hope on the horizon. I remain confident that we will eventually settle into a fair and reasonable place. I see signs where patients truly are at the center of the system once again; and quality, safety and costs stabilize for everyone.

Darla's Story

Darla's story is an important part of why I left a successful career as an ICU nurse. She made me see modern health care in a whole new light. After my experience with Darla during her medical crises, I realized how far modern health care has drifted.

Without a doubt, Darla's experience brought the stark reality of marketing, money and the hierarchy of power in large corporations to the forefront…for me. This experience left me in no doubt about the dangers to one's career if you aren't high enough on the professional food chain to influence the bottom line for the powers that be. Today, hospitals are so focused on statistics and the outward appearance to outsiders who hold the power to sway millions of dollars to the right or the left. It made me see how impotent we are, as nurses, when we see things go awry and have the audacity to call attention to them.

I never know which patients I will fall in love with, but Darla and her extraordinary family were so easy to love. Darla came to us when other hospitals told her to go home and get her affairs in order because her cancer was far too advanced to treat. She had a particularly aggressive form of cancer that had invaded her entire abdominal cavity. The metastasis was extensive and she came to us looking for hope. She underwent an aggressive surgical procedure that required her to be in ICU for several weeks and her course of recovery was fraught with multiple complications. She came close to bleeding to death on several occasions and I began to wonder why her episodes of hemorrhage were not investigated more carefully.

One day I approached her surgeon and asked why he had not sent her for studies to determine the origin of her bleeding. I asked him to, "Help me understand where you think the bleeding is coming from."

To say my inquiries were not well received, is an understatement. Without answers for his failure to investigate the cause of her hemorrhaging, the surgeon's only response was to take a defensive and angry stance. He began to sputter nonsensical justifications and made it very clear that a mere nurse was not to question his authority.

He would have been better off waving a red flag in front of a bull.

I am not afraid of physicians who get angry and defensive because I have always been just idealistic enough to believe that it takes a coordinated team effort to bring healing to any patient. I was married to a physician for ten years and I know that they are men and women just like we are: fallible, imperfect and trying to do their best to give their patients a second, third or even fourth chance at life. It takes a special kind of boldness to be a surgeon: to cut into another human being's flesh and slice into their inner parts, sewing and repairing broken organs infected with disease. I admire that boldness and courage greatly and have the greatest respect for the hundreds of fine surgeons I have had the privilege to work with closely.

Most doctors will tell you that a good ICU nurse is a surgeon's best friend, especially in community hospitals without residents on call while many times, working twenty-four hours per day. I love working with great doctors and I love making their job easier. It's a pleasure to take care of problems in the middle of the night so they do not have their sleep interrupted with minor requests. It's a great team experience and the mutual respect I have always enjoyed makes being an ICU nurse more fun than anything I can ever imagine. We get to save lives and make a difference in suffering people's lives every single day we go to work. It is hard work, but more fulfilling than any job the hospital has to offer, in my opinion.

On this particular day, the doctor I was talking to did not exactly welcome my questions, or the threat that they posed to his position. To this day, I never understood why he did not come to the unit when she was bleeding. I will never understand why he didn't try harder to get to the root of her complications earlier until he was ultimately forced to do so. Did it have anything to do with the fact that she was African American? I would hope not, but there are indeed evidences in hospitals around the country that black patients do not receive the most aggressive treatment. Darla was a highly successful and beautiful woman, a banker, with devoted and educated children who stayed at her bedside for weeks. They kept careful notes and asked questions constantly.

This was a beautiful family, one that I got to know well over her many weeks' stay in the ICU. When she had several episodes of hemorrhaging that caused her to vomit quarts of blood, her hair would become matted with blood, and her body would be severely weakened by the trauma involved in resuscitating her. I remember several times when I would wash her hair, bathe her and lovingly apply lotions and creams to make her feel and look beautiful again after such episodes. The final ritual involved putting on her makeup and inserting her special signature gold hoop earrings back in place. She was a dignified woman and it was important to help restore her dignity after her medical crises.

I learned many years ago how important the "little" things are to patients. When nurses take the time to show loving kindness to their patients, it speaks volumes regarding their worth and value;

I truly believe it helps people find comfort and healing in the midst of the worst of medical crises. Care and comfort is woven into the fabric of who nurses are; it's just as important as any of the technical or assessment skills we possess. It is one of the reasons why nursing has ranked at the top of the Barna research polls for decades as THE most trusted profession by the public.

When I challenged the doctor on this particular day, he was angry enough to contact hospital administrators. Next, he directed his mid-level support staff to transfer Darla to another floor the following day. Later that afternoon, Darla's daughter came up to the ICU and pleaded with me for help. "I'm afraid Mommy is going to die, Teri! Her blood pressure is 60/40 and she has been lying in bloody stools for the last half hour. The nurses don't have time to clean her up. Please help us!" I assured her that something would be done and contacted my nurse manager for help in returning her to the Intensive Care Unit.

After going downstairs and talking with the medical team, she returned and told me the doctor was not willing to bring her back to the ICU, there was nothing more she could do. My mind was racing now because I knew I would have to "buck the system," or stand by and do nothing. I knew that the director of nursing was out of town that week, so my only recourse was to go to a higher level of authority for help. I sat down and wrote an email to the hospital's CEO, asking that the risk management department become involved. Hospital risk managers are in charge of "damage control" when things go wrong. We needed administrative support to help manage this situation and make sure that appropriate measures were taken to ensure appropriate care.

That same day, Darla's medical situation continued to be unstable, and her daughter came back to the ICU in tears, asking again for help. I pulled her into an empty room and said to her, "Crystal, if this was my mother, this is what I would do: I would ask the surgical team to take your mom to CAT scan to investigate the source of her bleeding, and return her to the ICU again. If they are unwilling to do that, tell them that you are going to talk to hospital administration and the risk management department. I know that my job will be in jeopardy if they find out that I told you to do this, but I don't care. We have to get your mom back to the ICU."

Things began to happen after she followed through. I was called to go and take Darla to the CAT scan department and to the interventional radiology department, where testing showed that she had a splenic artery aneurysm that could not be accessed by catheters needed to place a patch upon the bleeding blood vessel. During the three-hour procedure, I stayed by Darla's head and prayed with her, explained what was happening and speaking words of comfort and encouragement to her constantly. The procedure was long and arduous, and the wonderful physicians tried everything possible to stop her bleeding. After we were done, I got her ready to transport back to the ICU and rushed her back upstairs, since her blood pressure was still dangerously low in spite of medications and blood transfusions given during the procedure.

As we wheeled her into the Intensive Care Unit, Darla suddenly sat up in the cart and started vomiting massive quantities of blood, with clots as big as my hand. She became cold and clammy and we rushed her into the hospital bed and called a CODE Blue. The entire medical team arrived and she was intubated, placed on life support and the blood bank notified that we needed as much blood as they could provide for her ASAP.

The surgeon was now at the bedside, screaming orders and pacing back and forth, yelling at us to go faster as we hung blood products, poured in IV fluids and vasopressors needed to save her life. For the next three and a half hours we worked feverishly to save her. We gave her over thirty units of blood products and multiple medications, including pain medication and sedation to help her stay calm during the crisis. At one point, I gave a narcotic to her in her IV and turned around to hang another unit of blood, forgetting to return later to sign out the medication with the computer scanner. Later on, you will see how that small distraction almost cost me my job.

Darla made it through that day and she stabilized in the ICU over the next week. The family requested a care conference with the entire medical team to determine the next course of action. We had the team meeting in the administration department of the hospital and the surgeon's partner arrived to explain the plan of care and answer the family's questions. He was a wise and thoughtful man and explained her condition and our options carefully, which satisfied the family. Unfortunately, Darla's aneurysm was in a unique spot that was difficult to get to non-surgically and she was not stable enough to go through another major surgical procedure. The hospital agreed to have an outside specialist consult and explore other options for treatment, but this ultimately did not resolve her challenging condition.

The family walked away from that meeting with a better understanding of her complex situation, satisfied with the answers they received that day. They thanked me for arranging for the meeting and told me later that the only reason they did not seek a medical malpractice attorney's help was because they trusted me and all that had been done to find a way to help her. Sadly, Darla died a couple of weeks later after a final massive bleeding episode. By then, the family had decided that she should not be put on life support again since her condition was not treatable. She died on my day off that week and I grieved for a war that was ultimately lost after many battles to save her life.

The following day I returned to work and before the family left the area, they came to the hospital to say goodbye to me and thank us all for working so hard to save Darla. As I embraced her daughter, she whispered in my ear that she wanted me to have a small gift to remember them by. She pulled me aside and asked me to close my eyes and hold out my hand. I did so and she placed a small package in my palm. When I opened my eyes, I saw that she had given me Darla's special earrings: a set of gold hoops that we had put on after every time we had cleaned her up from her bleeding episodes. They were a beautiful reminder of Darla's smile and happy times we had spent together during her stay in the ICU. I cried and cried and thanked Crystal for this special gift, given in love from the heart that would remind me thereafter of why patient advocacy is so important.

Today, I call these my luck earrings and wear them every time I am asked to speak in public. This small ritual helps me remember constantly why I do what I do. I am a professional nurse advocate and I will persevere with all my future clients to speak up on their behalf, using my experience and expertise to help them stay in the center of the model of care, always.

A couple of weeks after Darla died, I was working hard to save the life of another patient in the ICU who was also bleeding postoperatively. He was a lovely gentleman and I was talking and laughing with him as I explained our plan for the day, hanging several units of blood. My nurse manager called me out of the room and told me she had been asked to escort me to the Occupational Health department. What for, I wondered? I was healthy and this was an inconvenient time since I was busy with my patient who needed another unit of blood.

She told me that I needed to do a "urine drop" exam, since I had been accused of stealing narcotics. One of the doses of pain medication had not been properly scanned out during Darla's CODE Blue weeks earlier and they had to make sure I was not using narcotics; stealing drugs from a patient. One of the surgeon's assistants had found my error and reported it to administration. I stood there with my jaw dropped open, wondering if they had lost their mind. I had been the hospital's top ICU nurse for decades. I showed none of the classic signs of a drug-abusing nurse. I had taken the most difficult cases for years, the VIP's, the most challenging assignments. I was a nurse mentor, educator and leader. Patients had sent multiple letters commending me to hospital administration. How could they really think I would do something so heinous after knowing me so well for so many years? I don't know whether I was more shocked or more insulted that day.

As my manager escorted me to the Occupational Health department, I remember shaking my head in disbelief, telling her over and over again that this was so wrong, so unkind, and so unfair. It slowly dawned me upon that this really had nothing to do with anyone truly thinking that I was a nurse addict. The point was being made that I should NEVER go up against a physician who made millions of dollars a year for the hospital. When it comes right down to it, whom is a hospital going to side with when a nurse blows the whistle? Nurses are, in the long run, expendable. Talented, high profile doctors who make a lot of money for hospitals are much less easy to lose. Point taken.

After all is said and done, this doctor actually did me a great favor. My 10-day suspension from work (why does it take ten days to get a urine screen back?) gave me a valuable opportunity to review my career direction and my options for the future. I remember telling my husband that week, in the midst of tears, anger and hurt at what I was going through, "NO ONE will ever tell me again that I cannot advocate for a patient!" I carefully investigated patient advocacy programs around the country and signed up for one in Arizona that specifically trained experienced nurses in the business of professional advocacy. The trajectory of my career was changing, thanks to a very painful experience at that hospital. That pain was a gift in disguise.

Tips to Equip: Getting more help when you just know "something isn't right"

1. Physicians and specialists have been trained to practice in an area of expertise that is on a higher level, so it's very difficult to question their knowledge, authority or recommendations. However, when you know that there may be more to be done for you or the loved one you're advocating for, don't just settle for their word–especially if your gut is telling you differently.

2. Communication is key, the right communication, which is as polite and respectful as you would expect in return, but that doesn't mean bow down to their opinion if you feel strongly that more needs to be done. After all, they are in the *practice* of medicine, which means they aren't perfect either.

3. When all else fails, resort to going up the hospital food chain to achieve the results you need. Ask for a meeting with risk management and a care team. This lets the facility know you are an advocate for yourself or your loved one and your concerns won't be easily dismissed simply because you don't have clinical credentials.

~~ Section II ~~

Private Professional Patient Advocates: Another Level

In this section, you will become more familiar with the term, Private Professional Health Advocate. There are various levels to patient advocacy, but this book will help you understand the difference between the different types of advocates. There are those who have your best interests at heart and there are those whose loyalty lies somewhere else. By the time you finish reading this section, you will realize just how easy it is to figure out the best advocate for your needs and how it can make all the difference in the outcome of the situation you (or your loved one) may be facing. Pay close attention in the following pages because the requirements for each type of need is different; and truly, you are the best one to decide which type of advocate will be the best fit for you.

This chapter goes into great detail about private professional health care patient advocates and the level of detailed care they can provide. A wonderful illustration is depicted in, "My Caregiving Journey," by Kate Curler. I have asked Kate Curler to tell her story here from the perspective of not only a legal professional in the advocacy field; but also as a family member when she found her voice in advocating for her parents. Kate is one of Chicago's very finest legal patient advocates and she does her best work in some of the halls of skilled nursing facilities in the Chicago area. Kate knows where the best and worst facilities are and it is a high compliment if she moves one of her clients to one of the better ones. Kate is a friend, a valuable colleague, and a funny, engaging person who can make the most depressing situations manageable once she steps up to advocate, particularly for seniors. We work together well and she has taught me so much about the U.S. justice system.

You also need to understand the other types of advocates out there in order to distinguish, without a doubt, the types who are for you and "the others." Briefly, hospital advocates have a loyalty to preserve the best interests of the hospital that pays them. Their job is to ensure that risk is minimized for the hospital and its staff–particularly on the clinical side. Insurance company advocates are paid by the insurance company, therefore they must look out for the best interests of the insurance company. Their job is to ensure that, in plain English, all of the administrative pieces are put in place to absolve the insurance company of monetary responsibility, whenever possible.

For instance, if a patient receives costly medical care with an out of network provider, the advocate may be on the claims and/

or denials team to help decide if the treatment, all or partial, was medically necessary. Is there any way the patient can bear some of the financial responsibility, even if the treatment was completely necessary? Will the insurance company cover the costs incurred by the patient? Should they take the loss or ask the patient to pay for a portion?

It's very easy to see which type of advocate you do NOT need, but it can be a challenge to decide the level of expertise you need once you decide you need a private professional patient health care advocate. Within the pages of this book, you'll find the answers to help you make practical decisions that serve your best interests, and only yours.

Chapter 2

What is a Private Professional Health Care Advocate?

What Exactly is a Private Professional Patient Advocate?

Private professional health advocacy is a young, but rapidly growing profession. In broad terms, a professional patient advocate is focused on three main priorities: quality care, preventing medical error, and protection of patient rights. Advocates can also save clients thousands of dollars when negotiating with insurance companies, not to mention saving lives and bringing peace of mind to families in crisis. Besides helping patients, professional advocates benefit hospitals by reducing readmissions, preventing medical error, and providing improved communication and education to families in medical need.

At the present time, advocates can come from many different walks of life and educational backgrounds. There are certificate programs (as opposed to a degree program) in patient advocacy offered at a few large universities for people desiring to enter the field. Please don't misconstrue an advocate who has completed a "certificate program" at a university to mean that the advocate has taken a written "certification exam" that tests their knowledge and skills. There is presently no national accreditation examination for private patient advocates, though it's in the development stages now.

If you do an online search for patient advocacy, there are two main advocacy associations that will frequently appear. They are NAHAC and the APHA.

Trisha Torrey founded the APHA, or Alliance of Professional Health Advocates, in 2009. According to their website, the goal of the APHA is, "to help private, independent advocates start and grow successful practices, to help them maximize their reach, and therefore maximize patient success." (Alliance of Professional Health Advocates, 2016) They boast of a membership of over 550 private, independent advocates. The APHA has an online directory called, AdvoConnection, where the public can search their database of members.

NAHAC, the National Association of Health care Advocacy Consultants (NAHAC) was also founded in 2009. NAHAC also has an online database of members, the *National Directory of Health care Consultants* that the public can utilize when searching for an advocate. Here is what NAHAC has to say about their organization: (NAHAC, 2015)

- We promote rigorous standards for the practice of advocacy including ethical considerations and codes of conduct when providing medical decision-making support;

- We educate consumers and health care professionals on research and current trends in patient-centered navigation, advocacy and decision-making support;

- We partner with individual advocates and other grassroots organizations to collaborate on patient-centered reforms that maximize use of the health care system, protect consumer choice and improve access to high quality, affordable care

In 2009, NAHAC developed an advocate Code Of Ethics. They have also recently developed a set of recommendations called Best Practices and Standards that will be a first step in developing a national accreditation process. These guidelines were presented at the NAHAC national conference held in Chicago in October 2014. The two main advocacy associations (NAHAC and APHA) collaborated to decide what qualifications shall be required of professional patient advocates in the future as well as what the testing and national accreditation process will look like.

The Patient Advocacy Certification Board (PACB), the organization charged with developing a certification exam for patient advocates, summarizes the roles that patient advocates play in this way: (Patient Advocate Certification Board)

- Provides services to patients as they navigate the health care system,

- Works directly with patients to ensure that they have a voice in their care,

- Works to make sure that patients have sufficient information to promote informed decision-making,

- Plays an informational role,

- Is committed to helping patients make informed choices and access resources,

- Ensures that a patient's wishes are the guiding force behind decisions affecting medical care and the withholding of care, and

- Collaborates effectively with other members of the health care team

It is also important to understand what an advocate *cannot* do for you. The first ethical standard developed by NAHAC is very clear that advocates will not be the providers of direct medical care. It states, advocates "shall not recommend specific treatment choices, provide clinical opinions, or perform medical care of any type, even if they possess clinical credentials. (Patient Advocate Certification Board)

From my perspective as a nurse advocate, medically trained and experienced advocates are still the advocates of choice. A 2014 Gallup poll (Gallup, 2014) found that eighty percent of Americans believe that nurses have "very high" or "high" standards of honesty and ethics. Nurse advocates with strong clinical backgrounds are street-smart and savvy about where to go in hospitals to have our client's needs met. We review medical records and see red flags in charts that the average nonmedical client would never catch. We know how to stand up for our clients and how to interact with medical professionals in a nonthreatening way to get what our client needs, keeping them at the center of the health care system's model. We see it all, we know the danger spots and we thoroughly understand patient rights. We know who to speak to in hospitals to get the most appropriate attention and we understand the hierarchy of health care in a way that the general public does not. Typically, we are experienced as advocates from the onset because we have protected our own families and friends when they were going through health care crises as well.

While the reality is that everyone needs an advocate in this world of modern health care, we have seen many different reasons that people do NOT hire an advocate when they are experiencing health care or elder care transitioning crises. I think the most common reason is because most people do not even know the industry exists, or what value we provide for patients and families. The second most often reason is price. People are still in shock from all of the increased out of pocket expenses they are experiencing since the Affordable Care Act came into law. Everyone I know will agree that there is little that is affordable in this new world: higher costs for insurance, higher deductibles, fewer doctors and dentists who can take Medicaid patients, continually rising costs of health care, etc. I get it, as my own insurance premiums have skyrocketed in recent years, and the future looks very dismal. I was asked recently on a business news TV program if I thought it was all a big scam by the insurance companies. I told the reporter that I doubted it very much. When Blue Cross Blue Shield loses 480 million dollars in one year, they have no choice: premiums HAVE to rise! It is simple math. Here in Illinois, all four major carriers are requesting the government allow 41 to 53 percent increases next year in insurance premiums. This is a scary time for health care in America!

One of the most common family dynamics I see when parents start to fail is for one child (usually a daughter) to step up and do most of the caregiving, going to doctor appointments, arranging mom or dad's appointments, paying their bills and managing all the various problems that arise when parents age and stubbornly insist upon living in their own home until they die, whether it is safe to do so or not. As the time commitments increase (while said daughter is trying to run her own family, job, etc.) she starts to get frustrated, stuffing her anger and becoming sarcastic about the other siblings who won't step up and help her. At this point she does not even realize that her burnout is starting to make her come across as a strident martyr, and she alienates herself from the rest of the family who cannot or will not step up to help. The daughter often tells everyone she knows long stories about how she suffers alone with no one else to help and cries that no one else will help so she "has to do it all." To this woman, I would say as kindly as possible, "You don't HAVE to do everything at all; it is your choice." There is help available on many fronts, whether you have financial resources or not.

Aging parents will often hear things from an outsider (especially a nurse) in ways they cannot hear the same message from a child. They are afraid of appearing weak, or being treated like a child from their own children. I remember the last time my dear father came to visit me in Chicago. He was 74-years old and a helpful flight attendant asked if he could get his bag out of the overhead compartment. My father retorted, "What do you think I am? Feeble or something?!" We laughed about that for years, though not to his face.

Our parents' pride hurts, even though deep down they know they are failing and cannot stay in their own home alone forever. The thought of moving is frightening, overwhelming and they fear they will not have the money to afford a comfortable place. Often they hope they will die suddenly and avoid the calamity altogether. But then there are consequences after the death: guilt, anger and regrets that families must deal with for years, wondering if they did all they could. There is help available; and a wise advocate can help families walk through the complexities of choices, estate planning, financial strategies and the various options for people with limited income. Yes, there is a cost to hire a private advocate, but what about the cost of missteps along the way, medical error, early infirmity, and the very real possibility of death brought about by accidents? What is the cost of losing our parents or loved ones before we have to? Everyone has choices, different levels of financial abilities and family members who can share the burden; then there is the willingness to ask for help. As I said earlier, there are no "do-overs" with our parents. Our family was lucky to have an ICU on that cruise ship in Belize, so we are now in our ninth extra year of having Papa with us. Was it worth it? Undoubtedly, even if they paid for my services, which they did not. Papa has been able to experience the joy of five extra grandchildren being born, and he is now the primary caregiver for his wife Ramona, whose health has since deteriorated. Family is important and it really does "take a village" to surround our aging parents with all they need. Professional advocates can seamlessly become a part of the village that is engaged to help keep our parents around and healthy for as long as possible.

Whether you learn to do the job yourself or hire a professional advocate, one thing is certain: everyone needs a health advocate these days! It's a strange time in the U.S. health care system. I know I personally can't fix a broken, unfair system, but I can use my years of clinical experience to help people navigate it as safely, efficiently and as economically as possible—one person at a time. That's why I tell people I have the greatest job in the world. I can make things possible that people are unable to do on their own simply by talking to the right people, asking the right questions, and standing up for what is right, just and fair. Someday I will be old (hopefully) and feeble, and in need of the kindness and skill of others who will help me get better in the hospital. I hope that someone will be there for me. This job, this amazing privilege of being a private professional health care advocate, is not really a job; it is a calling. And right now I am hoping that when I get there, the health care system in America will have undergone some healing of its own.

A Nurse Advocate Steps In

Here's a good example of a case where a nurse advocate stepped in to help a family member determine if his aging mother's living situation was really the best option for her. Because he didn't know what she needed and he wasn't really sure how to help her, he contacted a nurse advocate for assistance, which was ultimately the best choice in advocates due to the clinical expertise needed to help make the right determination for the patient.

A loving son contacted us to evaluate his elderly mother who lived in a senior housing development with a full-time caregiver in the home. His mom had recently fallen, and he wanted to know if this was a safe situation, or should the family start looking for a skilled nursing facility. Upon meeting her, I realized that, despite her physical limitations, this dear woman had a very clear preference to stay in her own home, with live-in caregivers. All of her friends were living in that building. Her bridge groups and even her doctor were there in the same building. I could see that she got around quite well with her walker, and she was clearly competent to make her own decisions. I told her son that I felt this would be a much better living situation, and with some adjustments in her plan of care and a review of her medical plan with her physician, she would likely live a longer, happier, and even safer life in her own home for quite some time.

One of the alarming things I noticed when I reviewed this woman's medication list was a surprising number of prescription medications that have side effects of dizziness, weakness and loss of appetite. Overmedication of seniors is a serious health hazard and is particularly dangerous in cases where the person is seeing multiple doctors. In the rush of quick office visits, many doctors do not take the time to carefully review the entire medication list. And then there's the issue of professional courtesy: doctors are often hesitant to discontinue medications that another physician has prescribed. This particular woman was taking 14 medications, three of which were psychotropic drugs, though she denied any history of mental illness. I have seen far too many seniors fall and break a hip or sustain a fractured skull secondary to probable medication-related issues. Broken bones in the elderly often have tragic domino-effect deterioration in other systems. For those who are discharged from a hospital to a local rehabilitation facility, the risk of acquiring a hospital, or nursing home-related infection may cause a multitude of other health problems, and even result in fatality.

Teri Dreher

Most people who hire a PPHA are amazed at all the ways that we help, not only the patient, but the family as well. Just as I have told my own family members: if a mom is able to stay at home with her children when they are young, it is a choice they will never live to regret. There are no do-overs with our children when they are young; we will never get those years back. The same is true with our parents. Though none of us has perfect parents, when they are old and becoming feeble, they need our help. If we can stop and put our own careers on hold to help them, and if we do that with great love, tenderness, and skill, we will never regret those years. Our own children will watch how we respect and value our parents, and that is how they will treat us when our time comes.

But for those adult children who are unable or unwilling to put their lives on hold to attend to their aging family member's needs, the next best thing (and sometimes the even better thing) is to hire a PPHA. An advocate will watch over their care, go to doctors' appointments, review their medical records, and, if admitted, a PPHA will go to the hospital, review the medical records, and ask all the tough questions. They will arrange for the right kind of home care services and even negotiate and resolve billing and insurance problems. Our clients tell us all the time that there has never been a time in U.S. history when our services are more needed, and I must agree after walking this path with family members many times before. Investing time, money and care into helping our parents as they age is some of the best-spent money a family will ever spend. There are no do-overs where family is concerned!

PPHAs are paid consultancy fees by the patient or their family, typically $125-$200 per hour, to work within "the system" to achieve better outcomes for their clients. Neither Medicare, nor private insurance will cover the cost of advocates.

My Caregiving Journey by Kate Curler

My personal experience as a caregiver and advocate for my parents was a journey of over 10 years. This experience brought me to the realization of the importance for caregivers to have a strong advocate and led me to launching my business, fighting for my clients. I now have a law office which offers legal services to seniors, the disabled and their families, provides advocacy services for my clients to get the best care in nursing homes as well as the best chance to access services and resources to go home. I also work closely with caregivers to put plans together for loved ones. I have a true passion for this work and love what I do.

My mother, Deborah Curler, was diagnosed with Type 1 (juvenile) diabetes at age four in 1952. At that time, her life expectancy was 50 years of age. She eventually lived to 64 years of age, but she struggled with health issues for her last decade. In 2003, I lived in Northern California, but I decided to move closer to my parents in Bay City, Michigan. I got a job as a prosecutor in 2003 and moved to Chicago.

My parents came to visit me in Chicago; and somehow my mother got E-Coli. She made it back to Bay City before she became ill, but ended up in a septic coma for a period of weeks. I took a leave from my job and sat bedside for her, with my father,

Ronald Curler. After her doctor's told us repeatedly she would not survive, she woke up one morning. Her condition was bad. My mother had nerve damage and could barely move her arms and legs. There was only one good rehabilitation center in my hometown of Bay City and I desperately wanted her to go there. The discharge person at the hospital told me this was not possible, as my mother did not have insurance to cover her for this facility. I learned firsthand the importance of advocacy and not taking, 'no' for an answer when the proper care for a loved one is at stake. I clearly told the discharge person her answer was not going to work for my mother and we needed to get to a better solution. I wanted someone to call the insurance company, whether she made the call or I made the call, to get to a different answer. She suggested I go get a cup of coffee with my father and she would work on it. I wasn't sure if this was just a trick to get rid of us and was pleasantly surprised security did not escort us out. When I came back, a different solution was possible as the insurance company was willing to pay for her stay as long as she improved. In the end, my mother and father worked very hard during the 17 weeks of inpatient and outpatient rehabilitation necessary for her recovery. Afterwards, my mother resumed all of her activities of independent daily living.

In 2007, my mother had a double bypass. Her heart was damaged from decades of diabetes. The hospital was unable to bring her out of anesthesia for a period of time and she lingered in a coma for a period of days. At the end of that week, she was not able to walk or move her arms enough to feed herself independently. I took another leave from work, this time from the private law firm where I worked. When she was discharged, my mother did not meet the medical criteria for the good rehabilitation center she had been in previously. My mother went to a nursing home for rehabilitation and a horrible one at that.

The first day, they mismanaged her food intake and insulin. She had a huge spike in blood sugar and she felt horrible. They took her for rehabilitation, but they only did some range of motion exercises with her and put her back in bed. My mother was only 59 years of age and I believed she would die there. My mother had worked too hard in her prior rehabilitation to have this happen.

Again, I advocated for my mother and looked for a solution to make things better. I talked to the administration and told them this care was not acceptable. I arranged for my father to monitor her blood sugar to help staff. I hired someone, a family friend and retired nurse, to assist in her care. Like my clients, I refused to let my mother be treated like any other person in that nursing home. I have learned that, when a client of mine is treated like any other resident in a nursing home, the care is usually horrible. I strive to have my clients treated like individuals and sometimes that means supplemental care in nursing homes. The person I hired to work with my mother got her up in the morning, made sure she was in the chair and had breakfast, and helped my father monitor her blood sugar. She also made sure my mother was back in her chair after rehabilitation and took extra steps to help her walk and move around in the evenings. Within three and a half weeks, my mother returned home.

On the second day of the nursing home, I returned to my job, now at a private law firm and only visited my parents for vacations for a while. However, my father was caring for my mother and like so many spousal caregivers, was stressed out and not caring for himself. In 2010, my father had an aneurism in his aorta, which is often fatal. I rushed back to Bay City and settled in for another hospital stay. I had a great job, with a bonus and partner opportunities. However, the stresses on my job were too great at this point from my parents' illnesses and I lost my job. Like too many American caregivers, I was forced to choose between caring for a family member, or focusing on my career. Against all odds, my father survived, but was legally blind, due to strokes in his eyes. Again, I kicked into advocacy mode and took him, twice, to a top eye clinic in Ann Arbor, Michigan and used creative solutions, like a homemade large print phonebook and a talking watch, to allow him to live independently.

I went back and forth between Chicago and Bay City, Michigan and looked for work. I had been a divorce attorney, so I looked in that field, but found nothing. I decided to work temporary jobs and move into the field of estate planning, probate, elder law and guardianship. I started doing tons of volunteer work and did what came naturally–fighting for my clients as I did for my parents. I reached out to resources, advocated for my clients to be treated better, looked for creative solutions and worked to treat my clients like individuals, deserving of respect. I was told over and over that this wasn't really elder law; this was something more. My parents and I continued to struggle as my father had a heart valve replacement surgery in 2011 and my mother, after being given the wrong dosages of a couple medications and a horrible hospital stay where I was unable to get to Bay City fast enough to help, passed away in January 2012.

I slowly realized that the business idea I had come up with, where you help people whether traditional legal services are needed or not, would not work in a traditional law firm. I decided to stop looking for work with law firms. I stopped all temporary work, and I launched the Law Office of Kate Curler in January 2013. I had put in time with a ton of volunteer work in the fields of aging and disability in the Chicago area. This work had also allowed me to form relationships with the best resources and facilities in the area.

I see myself as an advocate, who just happens to be an attorney. I feel blessed to do the work I do every day. I don't see the work I do as a job; I see it as an opportunity. My work honors my mother's legacy. My work means that my mother's hard work and dedication to living the best, independent life she could will result in that same life being lived by my clients, through her daughter's hard work and dedication.

The Sandwich Generation

We are hearing more and more about the Sandwich Generation, a phrase coined to describe those who are caring for their children while also tending to aging parents.

The Sandwich Generation supersedes the Baby Boomers and Generation X because it includes all people with a parent over 65 who are also raising a child under 18 or financially supporting a child over 18. According to the 2013 Pew Research Study, 47 percent of people, aged 40-59 are members of the Sandwich Generation. (Pew Research Center, 2013)

When we think of people aged 40-59, we typically think of someone at the height of their career, working full-time, trying to pay their bills, providing for their children (or paying for college if their kids are over 18), while hopefully planning for their retirement. Adults of this age are very busy. Along with work, their kids may be heavily involved in sports or other activities that take up much of their free time. We're also seeing an increase in chronic medical and developmental issues with children born in the last 10 years. One sobering fact: scientists report that one in 68 children born in the U.S. today will be diagnosed with autism. (Centers for Disease Control, 2016) Add in the increasing numbers of children with life-threatening allergies and asthma, and many Sandwich Generation members have children with complex medical issues that require additional care, time, and financial resources.

Now let's look at the aging parent side of the "Sandwich." They, too, may require financial assistance, emotional support and extra care. According to the Pew Study, around 15 percent of middle-aged adults are providing financial support to their children and parents simultaneously, while 73 percent of middle-aged adults surveyed by Pew have provided financial assistance to their children over 18. (Pew Research Center, 2013) We hear about these issues all the time with our clients: For her safety, Mom really needs to move to a memory care facility, but it costs $9,000 a month and Medicare won't cover it. Dad desperately needs a new set of hearing aids, but they cost $5,000. The family house is 50 years old and needs a new roof, water heater, and furnace, but there is not enough money while paying for the nursing home. With people living longer, the costs associated with aging can be out of reach for many. Adult children can be caught in the middle, trying to pay their own bills and help their parents out financially at the same time. Pew found that 75 percent of respondents felt it an obligation to help their parents financially if they needed it. (Pew Research Center, 2013)

We cannot discount the time we need to spend with our children as well as our aging parents. Pew says that 68 percent of people aged 40-59 reported that their parents "frequently" or "sometimes" needed emotional support. Adding to the stress, 76 percent reported that their own adult children also needed support frequently or sometimes. (Pew Research Center, 2013)

Assistance with day-to-day living is a huge issue. According to Pew, 28 percent of middle-aged adults below the age of 60 reported one or both parents needing help with daily living. Thirty-one percent reported performed most of the assistance themselves; while 48 percent said they performed some of the assistance. When respondents to Pew's study were 60-years-old or greater, 50 percent of them reported a parent requiring day-to-day assistance. (Pew Research Center, 2013) Caregivers are expensive and hard to find—who will foot the bill? And in the case of hospitalization, the pressures are even greater as the adult child tries to balance being there with their parent at the hospital, talking to their doctors, trying to get information, all the while getting the kids to and from school, and hoping the boss will forgive the unplanned absence from work or decreased work performance.

When a parent's health fails, it is not uncommon for people to feel great stress and a loss of control, and we often see coping mechanisms that do not make sense at first glance. But the impending loss of a parent is a major life loss, and people are often surprised when otherwise normal family members begin to act out, either by becoming hyper-controlling, emotionally distant, passive-aggressive, or overly angry towards other family members. It is important to step back and remain calm, especially when major decisions need to be made as a family unit. Each family member should remain respectful of others and keep their dignity at all times; momentary lapses in self-control with one's words may have far-reaching consequences, not only for the present generation but for future ones as well. Children tend to repeat family patterns, so remember that every family member watches our example under stress carefully. Ultimately, people are judged not for their intentions, but by their actions and words.

Many years of working in hospital ICUs around the country have taught me one important thing: when family members behave badly in public, or react with anger, it is usually because they are more afraid than angry. Anger is a secondary emotion; the primary one is fear. Fear of losing a loved one can look different to each person, even in the same family unit. Whether a son or daughter is the firstborn, middle, or youngest child may be an important factor in how each one deals with death and dying. Previous losses and experiences with death also play a factor in how one grieves—or does not grieve—in the present moment.

I have found that listening is the most important thing that health care professionals or family members can do when confronted with an angry, emotionally distraught, or grieving person. If the anger has a just cause, the problem can often be addressed and resolved. If, however, the anger and lashing out at others is generalized, it may be a sign of great pain and can only be resolved through kindness, compassion, and a sincerely caring person sitting with the distraught person and hearing them. That is hard to find in today's fast-paced world of health care, but it is critically necessary. I remind myself often that the anger is not about me; it is because anger is much easier for people to deal with than grief. Anger feels powerful; admitting to deep grief and sadness makes people feel vulnerable, incapable and lost. Just being there for someone in deep pain is more important than most people realize. I often feel that our nontangible "deliverables" are just as important as the "wins" we cite when we work on families' behalf. We are a blanket of protection and safety, helping not only the patient/client, but the entire family as well. Every week I hear from family members who are stressed, burned out and frustrated with trying to manage everything on their own. I wish we could help more people who are struggling, but everyone must decide what value is when dealing with these complex issues. Unfortunately we often see people who have made "quite a mess of things" on their own before they realize they are in over their head and call us in.

Tips to Equip: Find the perfect advocate for your needs

- **Fees may be paid by the patient or their loved ones, but the "client" is the patient regardless of who is paying the fees.** To tell the truth, we sometimes experience some degree of ethical tension when we are hired by adult children to watch over their aging parents. At our advocacy firm, our nurses are always careful to point out that our client may be the one who pays the bill, but the focus of everything we do is centered on the patient, the one who is experiencing health care challenges. In most cases, the entire family agrees on a plan of care and how we support the patient. There are also times that we must work hard towards a collaborative plan that will meet the multiple needs of the patient. Be transparent with your prospective advocate. Ask how the needs of all involved will be met.

- **Professional advocates vary in their educational background and training.** Always ask about their credentials and experience when you interview them. It's important to know what your needs are before you hire an advocate. Perhaps you need someone simply to negotiate with your insurance company to pay your medical bills. You may not need a nurse or physician to help you with that type of situation, but you will need someone who has experience with insurance appeals. Perhaps you need a physician or nurse who has sharp clinical skills to oversee an entire medical crisis. Don't go looking for an advocate without a clear sense of what your family needs, and pay attention to your instincts when you meet the company representative. Ask about their experience with successfully advocating in situations similar to your own. Read the contract carefully before you sign on the dotted lines. Be sure and ask for a quote for services that you feel may be bundled together. Ask any questions that you can think of beforehand. Some private advocates will work alongside you and teach you how to be a more effective advocate yourself, saving you time and money in the long run.

• **There are also private advocates who are not in the medical field at all who call themselves private professional health advocates (PPHAs)—with questionable qualifications and very slick marketing campaigns.** In my opinion, some advocates are strictly business/marketing people who will charge large monthly maintenance fees to cover "all of your health care needs," though they lack personal mentoring or physicians or nurses working alongside them who know what good health care looks like. Ask lots of questions about experience and education. Buyer beware! There is a difference between care managers and professional advocates: though professional nurse advocates can do complex care management tasks, care managers cannot always do effective advocacy. Nurse advocates have a wider scope of practice; and our businesses are not "corporate," but rather private, personal and very relational. It's not just what we do (tasks) that matters, it's how we make people feel when they have their own private nurse advocate watching over them. I have had clients tell me that hiring their own nurse advocate was the best gift their children ever gave them.

• **You may find hospitals and insurance companies that offer the services of their own "advocates" free of charge.** Why hire your own advocate instead of relying upon the hospital's patient advocate? One word: allegiance. Hospital advocates work for the risk management department of that particular hospital. Their job is to smooth out complaints and keep the hospital from being sued. Risk managers show up when doctors leave sponges in patients during surgery or when patients' families complain about quality-of-care issues. They get their paychecks from the hospital. Though they are great at handling small complaints and negotiating bills when sincere errors have been made, risk managers and hospital-based advocates are there for one reason: to save the hospital millions of dollars per year in legal fees and to protect the hospital's public image. The same is true for insurance company employees who call themselves patient advocates. Their job is to promote positive relations with customers while saving their company millions by not paying for claims they don't have to. Follow the money; that's how you will find who is really advocating on your behalf.

- **If you choose to advocate for yourself or your loved one, it is important to be watchful, vigilant, and present when doctors visit.** I tell all my clients how essential it is to have a small notebook handy so you can remember all of the questions you need to ask the nurse or doctor when you see them. Write everything down and keep notes on what different doctors tell you. Ask anything you wish, but be careful with how much time you spend—doctors often see around 20 patients per day, and they have the electronic medical records, orders, and reading of tests to do as well. Show respect and appreciation for good care as often as you can. Most patients would be surprised to hear that doctors, nurses, and other health care workers rarely get notes thanks or words of encouragement. People take us for granted, and a kind word can easily make our day!

Tips to Equip: Assistance for the "Sandwich Generation"

- Ask the village for help! They say it takes a village to raise a child. Befriend other parents who can help out with driving to baseball practice or transport to birthday parties. With 47 percent of adults in the Sandwich Generation, chances are good that there are fellow parents out there who will understand your need for help (and will probably ask for your help in kind!). Pay the neighbor's kid to mow the lawn while you spend some time catching up with your spouse. Take care of your bill-paying electronically, and schedule automatic payments so you don't find yourself with late charges.

- Take care of yourself, even in small ways, as often as you can. Sandwich "Generationals" can find themselves not eating properly, not exercising, and not taking time for themselves. While you may not have time for the gym membership, you can park the car further at work and get some extra steps in, or meet up with a friend and walk and talk on your lunch break. Mindfully choose healthier, yet still simple meals. There are many great options today, even at quick restaurants, if you don't have time to prepare a meal. Find hair salons that will cut your kids' hair at the same time you get yours cut.

- Talk to someone. If you find yourself stressed out, feeling sad, or not sleeping well, help can be a phone call away. If dear friends are also busy like you, there are website therapists who will Skype with you over the phone, rather than having to drive to an office. If you're affiliated with a church, talking with a respected clergy member can help as well.

- Consult with a private professional health care advocate (PPHA). A PPHA can do a wide variety of things to help you keep your parents healthy and safe. For example, they can help manage your parents' medical care, facilitate communication between physicians, organize medication management and suggest devices that will make living on their own easier and safer. If you're not sure, a PPHA can help assess whether parents are safe to live on their own, or suggest high-quality senior living communities that are within their budget. They can also help you navigate the complex world of Medicare and insurance concerns.

Know Your Rights

Do you know your rights as a patient, from a legal standpoint? Your rights go well beyond the HIPPA (Health Information Privacy and Protection Act) laws governing the privacy of your personal information.

This section, in many ways, is a continuation of section II as it highlights the value a PPHA can add to your health care experience, especially as it pertains to helping you *exercise* your rights.

It may seem like a lot of mumbo jumbo, but when it comes down to it, knowing the law as it pertains to your rights in each of these situations is crucial to your survival to ensure that you are well informed, which helps ensure that you receive the proper treatment to improve your quality of life from a health care perspective.

After you finish reading this section, you will be prepared to advocate on your own behalf, in many ways. At the same time, after you finish reading this section, you will also be prepared to know if the private professional health care advocate you've chosen to carry out your wishes is up to the task at hand. I share a portion of William's story here to show you exactly how a PPHA played a significant hand in helping him exercise his rights, which ultimately improved the quality of his life, and I firmly believe, *saved* his life.

You will find that even if you don't remember word-for-word the law as it relates to your rights, the information in this section will help you become familiar enough to know when something "just isn't right," or you have the feeling something is being overlooked.

You've probably overlooked the large banner posted in almost every hospital you've ever visited. It is titled, "Patient Bill of Rights" and it is usually prominently posted in the hallway of the hospital. Because it is so unobtrusive, most of the time, you may see it, but not really "see it."

That poster is chock full of valuable information that can help you as you navigate your way through a hospital stay; an unexpected procedure the doctor wants you to have right away; your rights as it relates to waiting until you feel fully informed versus being ambushed to have a test you're unsure of; requesting a second opinion and a host of other privileges you're entitled to simply because you are the patient. After you finish reading this section, you'll never look past that poster again without giving it a closer inspection.

In this section, you will also hear about William's journey. The beginning of William's story is shared, in full, later on in this book, but this part of his health care journey is important to tell right here and now because it is a perfect example of patient rights being violated by well meaning hospital staff who did not have the full perspective of what a life lived out in a nursing home would mean to William, versus the freedom and health he would enjoy at home. This is a reason why advocates are important in telling "the rest of the story" to the healthcare providers. When an advocate understands hospital hierarchy, motivations, concerns with liability and can "speak the language" and get the win without going to court, it is a win, win for everyone.

Suffice it to know here that William had been back in the hospital again for almost a year after a serious medical condition occurred and we needed to help him and his family in a new and different way than we had done before. It's all about knowing what your rights really are, and who knows that better than a nurse advocate?

Chapter 3

The Patient Bill of Rights, Don't Leave Home Without It!

Knowing your rights as a patient is essential in order to exercise your rights! There have been many versions of a Patient Bill of Rights that have been circulated over the years. The truth is, our house and senate have never been able to pass legislation to adopt an official "Patient Bill of Rights."

In 2003, the American Hospital Association revised their original Patient Bill of Rights, and the AHA document formerly known as the Patient Bill of Rights has been revised and shortened and is now known as, "The Patient Care Partnership." (American Hospital Association) The AHA publishes a pamphlet bearing the same name, *The Patient Care Partnership*, which would ideally be given to patients at the beginning of their stay, although when casually surveyed, we couldn't find a patient who has ever seen this pamphlet.

Here are the tenets of The Patient Care Partnership taken straight from the brochure (American Hospital Association):

- **High quality hospital care** -- The AHA says that you have the right to medical care provided with "skill, compassion, and respect." (American Hospital Association) In turn, you have the obligation to inform your caregivers if you are in pain or you have concerns about your care.

- **A clean and safe environment** -- Clean and safe are broad terms. The AHA says that hospitals will use policies and procedures to keep you safe, and that if an "unexpected and significant" event occurs, you will be informed of it as well as any changes in your care as a result. There is more about this in chapter 5: *Dangers Lurking in Every Hospital.*

- **Involvement in your care** -- This is a very broad subject broken down by the AHA into the following subsets:

- **Getting information from you:** In order for the hospital to provide good treatment, you need to be open and honest about your past illnesses, surgeries, hospitalizations, past allergic reactions, and any medications and dietary supplements (vitamins and herbs) you are taking. You also need to inform them of your insurance status as well as any network or admission requirements that your insurance may have.

- **Understanding your health care goals and values.** You have the obligation to inform your doctor, care team, and your family of your health care goals and values. The hospital will consider your health care goals and values throughout your hospital stay.

- **Discussing your medical condition and information about medically appropriate treatment choices:** When you and your doctor discuss various treatment choices, you should be involved. You have the right to understand the various treatment options along with their risks and benefits, whether the treatment is proven or experimental, i.e. clinical trials, and what long-term side effects and/ or benefits you should expect from the treatment. You and your family have the right to know what needs to be done to take care of you after you leave the hospital. This extends into financial issues too; you have the right to understand the financial ramifications of receiving services not covered by your insurance, or using out-of-network medical providers. You have the obligation to tell your medical providers if you need more information about your treatment choices.

- **Discussing your treatment plan:** You have the right to consent or refuse a treatment plan. If you choose to refuse a treatment, your doctor should explain the consequences of refusing. You also have the right to participate or refuse to participate in a clinical research study.

- **Understanding who should make decisions when you cannot:** If you already have legal documents, such as a power of attorney for health care, or advance directives, please inform your doctor, your care team, and your family. If you need help in making difficult decisions, the hospital will have on hand a social worker and/or chaplain to assist you. Living wills and other lay documents do not carry the full weight that power of attorney for healthcare documents do. If people come in without a POA, the hospital has to guess who the surrogate decision maker should be if the person becomes unable to make their own decisions. Every person over the age of 18 should have a healthcare POA document, so that hospital personnel know who has legal rights to information as well a decisional capacity.

- Protection of your privacy
- Help with your bill and filing insurance claims
- Preparing you and your family for when you leave the hospital

High quality hospital care – The AHA talks about being treated with skill, compassion, and respect. A chilling piece of "insider information" is that if you are admitted through the emergency room without your own admitting physician, you will be "assigned" to the physician whose name is on the on-call list for the day. Yes, it is purely luck (good or bad) if you leave your choice of physicians up to the hospital. With so many physicians no longer seeing their own patients while they're hospitalized, in the case of hospitalization you will be assigned a hospitalist to oversee your care. A hospitalist is a physician who is employed by the hospital to take care of hospitalized patients. While they may be very good physicians, they do not know you, or your medical history (other than what you can provide). Having a stranger take care of you when you are at your sickest is fragmented care at its worst, and most dangerous. Ask most primary care physicians how they feel about not being allowed to manage their own patients in the hospital because they are handed over to hospitalists and you will hear mostly negative remarks; they do not want their patients managed by strangers either. It is the rare hospital today who will allow primary care doctors to come and manage their own patients. Sometimes the doctors are not even notified when their patient is admitted!

However, it's not a completely hopeless scenario as your involvement in your care can ultimately help improve the quality of the health care you receive no matter whom you receive it from. Many hospitalists are fine clinicians with excellent skills; the just do not have the long term relationship and allegiance that the patient's own doctor has for each patient, nor do they know what each patient's "normal" looks like.

- You are obliged to provide accurate information as to your diet, alcohol and tobacco habits, your symptoms, medications, vitamins, and supplements that you take, past medical history, past surgical history, and the different doctors that you see. A private health care advocate can gather this information for you and create a "medical profile" that you can bring to all of your physician's appointments. Having the correct information will help you get the most out of your physician appointments, and will improve the quality of your care.

Many patients are reluctant to tell their physician "everything" for fear that they will be judged. A frequent example is when it comes to admitting alcohol use. Patient J routinely drinks six cans of beer after work every day, but tells his doctor that he has two beers every Saturday night. When Patient J lands in the hospital after a car accident, the hospital physician is unaware that Patient

J is a "routine drinker," and after two days in the hospital Patient J goes into alcohol withdrawal ("DT's"), has multiple seizures, and ends up in the intensive care unit on life support. Alcohol withdrawal is no laughing matter! Doctors really need to know the real story so they can diagnose and treat early if patients start to go into delirium tremors, or alcohol withdrawal. Patients in DT's can become violent, hallucinate and even seize, so hospital personnel need to be prepared.

You have an obligation to share your health goals and values with your health care team as well as your family. This can be pretty difficult, because you may have vastly different goals than your health care team or than what your family wishes for you. Here's a common example: Patient L has just been diagnosed with cancer in her liver. Her family physician, after looking at her CT scan reports, gives her a grim outlook, but sends her off to see the oncologist all the same. The oncologist develops a chemotherapy plan and seems optimistic. The family is thrilled that the oncologist is so enthusiastic, and they are angry at the family physician for being so negative. The truth is, Aunt M trusts and believes her family physician, and really doesn't want to proceed with the chemo but does so because of her oncologist's encouragement and family's expectations. Aunt M decides that she will only agree to chemotherapy in pill form. She takes the pills for a few days and develops side effects that land her in the hospital with severe bleeding requiring multiple blood transfusions. After spending five days in the hospital, she declares to her doctor and family that she will never return to the hospital for any reason. She engaged hospice services at her home and had a very peaceful death two weeks later with her family beside her.

Throughout this section, there have been many areas discussed where a plethora of tips were shared, but I will summarize them for you in the *"tips to equip"* section organized by the topic discussed.

William's Story

After seven months of living at home with no infections and a much-improved quality of life, William developed an unexpected leak of cerebrospinal fluid, which led to a bad case of pneumonia. Once again, the problems began and over the course of the next year, he developed even worse strains of multidrug resistant, nosocomial infections. Nosocomial essentially means "acquired in the hospital," which is one of main reasons why we wanted to keep my friend out of the hospital: too many germs and a weakened immune system on his part, made worse by a nonstop onslaught of stress, pain, poor nutrition and an avalanche of "big guns" antibiotics over months and years.

A few months ago, I got another phone call from one of his sisters, saying simply, "Teri, we need you back again. They don't want William to come home and we're afraid he's going to die if we let them send him to another nursing home."

Two days later, I took the trip to the long-term, acute care hospital where he was being treated. I had been told that he was on the ventilator and that they had tried to wean him off several times unsuccessfully. When I saw him, he was on simple humidified oxygen to his tracheostomy and he was in no distress at all. I learned that the medical team was putting him back on the respirator every night, which I suspected was for the staff's convenience more than for the patient's benefit. He had recently been transferred to the main hospital after developing an airway obstruction from not being suctioned as often as he needed it. I was shocked to hear that he sometimes had to wait 20-40 minutes for someone to answer his call light. He was in the ICU section of the hospital. When I worked in ICU, the standard was always less than three minutes, at most, for attending a patient on a ventilator who needed help. His sister told me of other incidences where the facts of his case had been misrepresented.

When I spoke to his insurance nurse case manager, I learned that she was in the "Acceleration department" of the company. This man no longer met the criteria for a LTACH (long-term acute care hospital) and he was being advised to go to a nursing home that could care for his needs properly (ventilator and the many tubes and wounds). Unfortunately, the quality facilities with that level of experience would not accept him due to the complexity of his infection.

When I discussed his case at length with the insurance company case manager, I listed the many reasons why he would be better off at home: two full-time caregivers so he would never have to wait to be suctioned again; no hospital environment that would give him more infections; a trained, devoted sister who knew how to skillfully and aseptically care for his "trach," feeding tube, colostomy and wounds; and a special care bed that was better than the standard-issue hospital bed. The year prior, I had obtained the bed for him through insurance mediation. The bed was so high-tech that it continually rotated him slowly from side-to-side, preventing pneumonia and helping his bedsores heal. He would have all of this in addition to the immeasurably great comfort of being in his own home.

After telling her all of the medical reasons why I knew he would be better off at home, I also told her that he would have two advanced practice RNs on 24-hour care for him; a home health RN who was skilled at complex wound care and a home visiting physician who knew him well, and the family adored him. Lastly, I pointed out that the insurance company would save money by getting him out of a facility that was costing the insurance company at least $7-8,000 per day. By now, her excitement was palpable. She urged me to move full steam ahead and she would approve, "Anything we needed to get him home."

Unfortunately, the medical establishment was not so easy to convince; and they ultimately dug their heals in. They called for an ethics committee meeting. I enthusiastically agreed knowing I would have a full and impartial audience to make my case.

On the following Wednesday, I arrived with my complete medical profile, care plan and supporting documents. I was asked to wait in the hallway until they were ready 20-minutes later. I thought that was a bit odd, as there is really not supposed to be a "meeting before the meeting" on ethics committee hearings. When they finally admitted me, I saw that they had, in fact, not invited any impartial committee members. It was 12 of them from the hospital and me. The sisters had declined the chance to attend since they felt that their emotions could possibly get out of hand. They trusted me to represent their case well. I had talked to them about what they would and would not go along with, if a compromise became necessary. I knew the staff was going to tell me that he could only go home if he was discharged to hospice, under palliative care. My ace in the hole was a company in Illinois I found that would admit him under palliative care only, with no DNR order required. It was NOT hospice, though the parent company did have both hospice and palliative care divisions. They did not require a 'Do Not Resuscitate' order, as most hospice companies do.

During the ethics committee meeting, I first assured them that I was a career ICU nurse and I understood their hesitation in sending a patient with so many complications home. I told them that the family had hired me instead of an attorney because medical advocates know more about health care and patient's rights than most attorneys. I was there so that this case did not escalate into legal action.

As a nurse, I know that part of the big problem of costly U.S. health care is that the U.S. has far too many malpractice suits. This drives up the cost of health care for all of us. I listened to them, answered their concerns and laid out my solid plan as I had with the insurance company. I gave them a complete list of all 22 different facilities he had been in over the past three years. I listed the many complications, incidences of medical error and infections he had received. One facility had even broken his hip during a physical therapy session. I gave them all the reasons that his family and I believed, with all our hearts, that he would be safer and better cared for at home. I told them about the stress his sister had been under with the nonstop trauma over the past three years. I explained why they had good reasons, based in facts, not to trust the medical establishment.

As the meeting went on, I could see some of them starting to soften. The head of the ethics committee actually had some hospice experience and was familiar with the palliative care company I mentioned. When the doctor told me they would only agree to discharge if he went to a palliative/hospice company, I explained that the patient and family did not want to receive hospice services, but would agree to palliative with a full CODE order for pain management only. I could see that we had found a loophole.

One doctor, in particular, seemed particularly angry that I was there to oppose his plan, which was to transfer him to a skilled nursing facility. Honestly, for the doctors, they saw this as a huge liability issue. Doctors fear lawsuits more than anything, so they were cautious. I told him that I could not, in good conscience, suggest any of the awful facilities that were on the short list that would even accept him. He was disqualified from the better facilities because of the infection that this hospital had given my client. We simply had no better choice other than sending him home.

Since I knew the home environment and support he would have, I hoped that I ultimately allayed his concerns. He was still unhappy, however, he told me, "You are his advocate–it is your job to be honest with him and tell him he will die if he goes home!" I responded by reminding him that I was the patient's advocate, not the hospital's, nor the insurance company's advocate, and that I served the patient only. I would not have driven 2 ½ hours that day to address the ethics committee if I did not completely agree with my client and his family that he would be better off at home. Besides, I told him, "Even if he is ultimately going to die early from his condition, shouldn't he have the *right* to say where he will live out the rest of his days? Isn't that his *right to choose* where he lives?"

Silence covered the room for a few minutes. Then the head of the ethics committee, a physician, stood up and shook my hand and said, "Okay then, lets get him home!" There were smiles and handshakes all around after that and I left very pleased. We had won. It was a very good day indeed.

I later discovered the reason no outside members of the ethics committee were in attendance that day. They did not want impartial witnesses to be present at the meeting. The chief nursing officer took the meeting notes. Afterwards, there was a meeting after the meeting to decide what to document. They unfortunately documented things that were not true, saying that I agreed to have the family sign William out against medical advice. An AMA document opens up the family to be liable for costs not covered by insurance, and the insurance company had told the hospital weeks before that he would not be covered.

I had actually never experienced a hospital ethics committee lying before, but they must have been desperate. We still had several battles to fight before he came home. Fortunately, he did come home within a week and we all breathed a sigh of relief. I'm sure the doctors and nurses at the facility had never seen such a complex patient being sent home before, but the many advances in home health care management have made it possible to do things today that couldn't have been done even ten years ago. With the right support, including two standby advanced practice nurse advocates on 24-hour call for William, as well as the rest of our team, we knew he would be better off; he would live longer and he would avoid more of the infections and medical error that had already happened to him.

In this case, perseverance for patient rights paid off!

Tips to Equip: Take action if you aren't being treated with skill, compassion and respect

- Trust your instincts. We, humans, usually have a good sense of when things aren't going as they should. It's difficult to speak up when you're in a hospital bed. If possible, ask a friend or a loved one to be at your bedside, especially in the early mornings when most physicians make their rounds.

- Speak to your nurse about your concerns. Nurses usually know the individual physicians quite well, and may be able to give you insight or intercede on your behalf.

- When discussing your issues, try to explain your issues as calmly and kindly as you can to all concerned. That old adage is true; you always get more flies with honey than vinegar.

- You or a loved one should document your experiences on paper; include dates, times, and names.

- Many hospitals have their own "advocates" who are employees whose sole purpose is to keep patients happy so that they don't end up suing them later on. Ask for the advocate to come to your room and see if they can help you. Ask about their credentials: often hospital advocates are not even nurses but act as customer service representatives without any real knowledge of what a large or small problem entails from a medical perspective.

- If you have the courage and are feeling up to it, you could address the physician directly, or have a loved one address them for you.

- If those measures don't work, ask for the "charge nurse" in your unit. That is the nurse who is overseeing all of the nurses for that day.

- You can always request a different physician; there is usually even more than one hospitalist on duty.

- If you don't get anywhere with the charge nurse, you can then go "up the chain" and ask for the nursing supervisor; this is the nurse in charge of the nurses all over a particular hospital unit.

- The final approach is to ask your nurse for the phone number to risk management. This is the department in the hospital that handles lawsuits and potential lawsuits. Oftentimes just asking for their number will get you somewhere in the right direction.

Tips to Equip: Get involved in your care

- **Not too many patients question their doctor's treatment plan, but everyone should.** Treatment plans can be very complicated, and difficult to understand. Often, there may be more than one treatment option available, and you should understand all of them. This is another area where a private advocate who is medically trained can do a lot to advance your understanding of your treatment options. If an advocate isn't available to you, bring a loved one or a friend to listen and take notes; it is difficult for the patient to take all of the information in when you're thinking about your medical concerns!

- **Clinical trials may be an option.** A clinical trial occurs after a drug or device has been tested on animals. There are different "phases" of clinical trials, indicating how far along the medication or device has been studied. Doctors have to work with the Food and Drug Administration (FDA) on clinical trials; they cannot just decide to "invent" a new drug, procedure or a new device and try it out themselves. There is a definite process involved. Some clinical trials go very well, and new technology or medications become available to the public as a result. Other clinical trials are a disaster–a few patients die, or have severe complications–and the FDA calls a halt to that entire clinical trial.

Please don't discount the options of clinical trials; sometimes they may be your only, or best "chance" at improvement. There are times when patients are in a very fragile state, and their body simply cannot undergo a surgery that is routinely recommended for their condition. Here's an example: A woman had a very severe leaky valve in her heart. She desperately needed to get a replacement valve, but that would mean open heart surgery where her chest was sawed open, and her heart was just too weak to undergo the surgery. Fast forward—the doctor mentioned a clinical trial of a valve replacement that didn't involve sawing her chest open. It was still risky due to it being experimental and there were still the risks of anesthesia, but it was a much shorter anesthetic time and a much easier recovery without open-heart surgery. It was a tremendous success, and the woman made an excellent recovery and returned to a great quality of life.

We hear a lot about clinical trials for cancer drugs. When a patient has run out of options for treatment, they may decide to enroll in a clinical trial. The drug may help them, and they will definitely help others as well by allowing themselves to be part of the study.

- **Don't forget that you do have the right to refuse recommended treatment.** A woman went to her gynecologist for some abnormal bleeding. The doctor mentioned a hysterectomy to remove her uterus; that was all the patient heard. She signed the consent forms for the surgery, put a date on the calendar, and came back to her doctor for her preoperative physical. She cried to the medical assistant, "I don't want to have a hysterectomy, but he (the doctor) says I have to." The medical assistant shared the patient's concerns with the physician, and the surgery was immediately cancelled. The doctor prescribed some medications to help the bleeding. Fortunately the patient had the courage to tell the medical assistant her concerns about the surgery, and fortunately the medical assistant shared her concerns with the physician; that medical assistant was a health care advocate in that moment.

Refusing treatment doesn't mean your physician is going to agree with you, and he or she will probably try very hard to do their best to talk you out of it if they feel it is really not a good idea, but it is ultimately your decision. Emergency department physicians can relate many stories of patients who are brought in by ambulance (usually, after another person has called the ambulance), they are found to be having a heart attack and yet, for reasons of their own, they refuse treatment. As long as this patient has stable vital signs and a normal oxygen level, they appear to be thinking clearly, and are not intoxicated, they are usually allowed to refuse treatment after they sign an "AMA" form, the acronym for leaving the hospital "against medical advice." We as nurses and doctors may not agree with their opinion, and we do our best to inform and educate, but ultimately it is the patient's choice. On more than one occasion, those patients have been brought back to the hospital after having suffered a full cardiac arrest at home. It is important to know also that if a patient signs out AMA, the insurance company has the right to refuse to pay the bill in most cases, so the patient may be liable for many thousands of dollars of health care expenses. It is almost NEVER a good idea to sign out AMA just because you disagree with the doctors. Go up the chain of command and try your best to resolve the dispute or hire an advocate to fight on your behalf.

Tips to Equip: When you lose your right to refuse treatment

Here are some instances in which you will ***NOT*** have the right to refuse treatment:

- **You are a non-pregnant minor.** Pregnant minors are in a tricky and confusing situation. They can make decisions for their unborn child and they can make pregnancy-related decisions, such as consenting to an abortion. The pregnant minor, however, cannot make other medical decisions for themselves. For example, a pregnant minor cannot sign a consent form for an appendectomy. Their parent still has to sign for any non-pregnancy-related conditions. To muddy the waters further, a teenage parent can sign for their own child's appendectomy, however they can't sign for their own appendectomy unless they have been legally emancipated.

- **You have been declared mentally incompetent by a physician to make your own decisions.** Incompetence might be due to a number of different reasons that would include dementia, developmental delays, and mental illness. For example, actively suicidal patients would not be allowed to refuse admission to the hospital nor would they be allowed to leave the hospital. In fact, suicidal patients or any patient who is deemed to be a danger to themselves or others can legally be held against their will for a 72-hour observation, or even longer with the involvement of a judge. There are also situations of what we'll call temporary incompetence. An example of this would be during a surgery, for example, where the surgeon finds he or she needs to perform more extensive surgery or a different surgery than was originally planned. The patient, since they are or have been under the influence of general anesthesia, would not be considered competent to make the treatment decision until the anesthetic had been out of their system for 24-hours. In those cases, surgeons will approach the next of kin and discuss it with them. This is an example of why it is so important to have a durable power of attorney for health care, which is discussed in the "Legal Documents" chapter.

- **You have a current medical condition that is thought to impair your judgment.** For example, you're brought to the emergency room after a car accident. You have obvious serious injuries; you are acting inappropriately and at the same time, you are refusing treatment. Emergency department physicians will assume that you are currently incompetent to refuse treatment because you may have a head injury that has yet to be determined. The hospital will go ahead and treat you in a manner to which a competent person would have consented.

- **You are under the obvious influence of alcohol or drugs that impair thinking and judgment.** Emergency room physicians are quite familiar with intoxicated patients who are having a heart attack that was brought on by street drug use and who are not at all cooperative. Again, the physician will go ahead and treat the patient in a manner in which a competent patient would want to be treated. How is this done, you may ask? Doctors will use sedatives to gain a patient's cooperation. When they sober up and are advised that they were uncooperative and had refused treatment, they usually don't remember refusing treatment and are grateful for the care.

Tips to Equip: Do you need a PPHA? What type is best for your needs?

Here's where a PPHA would be of monumental importance. In the instance of a patient, such as William, who was unable to advocate for himself and his family could only do so much, finding a clinical private professional advocate who was enlisted to work on William and his family's behalf resulted in a successful outcome. A private professional health care advocate can:

- Understand complex medical situations and advocate on you or your family's behalf with hospital administration in a way that is more likely to have your case, not only heard, but resolved in a manner that is best for the patient versus looking out for the hospital's best interests

- Ensure that all of your health care needs are met in several ways. A PPHA can help clarify all of your options and ensure that you have access to the essentials needed for a successful outcome

- Protect you legally (while making sure your wishes/ rights are respected), in many cases, better than attorneys because they are more familiar with medical jargon that has legal implications

- Become your right hand supporter and patient care manager, talking with insurance companies to get additional benefits, arranging for proper medical supplies and care providers, overseeing the quality of care given by home health aides and home health care nurses, talking with your doctor and arranging complex documentation necessary for cost effective care, etc. We often have the time to spend teaching, being a 24-hour resource and guide that others cannot be in today's complex and fast-paced world of health care. As many patients have told us, "It's like having a nurse in the family!" As I have said before, it's the best job in the world for us as well

Chapter 4

Emergency Care
And Your Rights

A place you hope never to find yourself: The emergency room
What images come to your mind when you think of the emergency
room? For the ER inexperienced, it might be the ever-handsome
George Clooney playing the role of Dr. Doug Ross on the TV
series "ER." For others, the thought of the ER elicits palm-
wringing sweat and fear.

• The first issue you need to consider is whether to call an
ambulance. The decision to call an ambulance is never
taken lightly; most patients are worried about the cost,
and surprisingly a huge concern that most patients cite is,
"they don't want the neighbors to know what's going on"
by having an ambulance pull up in the front of the house.
Here's some very harsh reality, based upon the experience
of emergency department physicians.

◊ **In the event of any type of chest pain or
breathing difficulty, an ambulance should
always be called.** Emergency physicians cannot

count the number of times they have had to meet a deceased patient and their completely traumatized family member/driver in a private car parked at the entrance of the ER. The story usually goes something like this: "I wanted to call the ER, but he wouldn't let me." During a heart attack, a portion of the heart muscle itself is not receiving the blood (and therefore oxygen) that it requires, and the electrical wiring can be affected, causing a sudden and totally unexpected fatal-unless-treated-immediately heart rhythm known as ventricular fibrillation. Medical people call this lethal rhythm "v-fib," and the only really effective treatment for it is defibrillation, and it must be started within six minutes of the onset of this rhythm, or the patient's brain will suffer irreversible damage. If the heart attack victim is in a private car when this v-fib starts, there is *absolutely nothing* the driver can do to help the victim. Contrast this to the scenario of the same heart attack victim being in an ambulance. An ambulance has a trained paramedic in the back of the ambulance rig with the patient, and the patient is hooked up to the heart monitor. The moment that v-fib should begin, the paramedic grabs the defibrillator and at that moment has the best chance of "shocking" the patient's heart out of the lethal rhythm. Many successful "saves" have been made with the defibrillator readily available. You should also know that defibrillators are found in many public places now, and are simple enough for a second grader to operate. Most airports, sports stations, schools, bus stations, malls, grocery stores, and many places of worship will have defibrillators on hand. It is best that the operator have already taken a CPR course, but operating the defibrillator untrained is much better for the patient than doing nothing at all and waiting for paramedics to arrive.

◊ **In the event of any stroke symptoms, an ambulance should always be called.** Think of a stroke as a heart attack in the brain. In most cases, a stroke is caused by a blood clot that disrupts the flow of blood (oxygen) to the brain. In much fewer cases, a stroke is caused by a blood vessel that ruptures inside the brain, causing bleeding. The average layperson cannot tell the difference, and the action of a loved one will be the same: Call 911. There are many different symptoms of strokes, but some common ones are:

* Weakness on one side of the body, it may be just an arm or just a leg, or both an arm and a leg

* There could be slurred speech, or not making any sense when you are speaking

* There could be a drooping smile

* There could be passing out

Most people won't have all of these symptoms, or they may have totally different symptoms,

depending upon the area of the brain affected.
The best advice to give you is that if you're
not sure if it could be a stroke, but things just
don't seem right to you, it is better to call the
ambulance than not call them. So why do you
need an ambulance for a stroke? Many people
falsely believe that nothing can be done for a
stroke. These days, some hospitals, usually only
your major medical centers, can administer a
medication called a clot buster to break up a
large stroke. Now, this medicine isn't without
some serious risks, so it isn't used for "minor"
strokes, but may be tried on a major stroke
involving a large part of the brain. To qualify
to receive this clot busting medication, you
have to receive the clot buster medicine within
three hours of your symptoms starting. So if
you wait at home for a couple of hours to see if
the symptoms will get better, then you have to
spend time driving to the hospital, then you still
have to get into the ER, see the doctor, and get
the CT scan; by the time all of this occurs, you
may be outside of your three-hour window for
treatment. If you call the ambulance at the onset
of the symptoms, you stand the best chance for
treatment of a massive stroke.

◊ **In the event of any medical issue that appears to
be an immediate threat to life or an arm or leg,
an ambulance should always be called.** The old

adage, "Better safe than sorry," certainly rings true in medical emergencies.

- If time permits, grab the "important documents." This is especially true for someone who has ongoing medical problems, or is in the middle of a complicated treatment, such as cancer treatment, or who has had a lot of medical problems in the past. The important documents should be kept together, "ready to go" in the event of a call to 911. You will receive faster and more skilled care with the presence of these documents. The ER physician won't spend all of their time looking for your records; they will instead be spending the time looking at you. The important documents would include:

  ◊ A list of all current medications, their strength, when they're taken, what they're for (every empowered patient should have a general understanding of what each medication is for) and who prescribes it. This list should also include vitamins and herbal supplements, as some of them will interfere with or have a harmful interaction with medications that may be given at the hospital

  ◊ A list of all the physicians that you see, along with their phone numbers

  ◊ A list of all allergies—medications and foods. Along with the allergy, have written down what your allergic reaction is. Some unpleasant side effects of medication are called allergies by some patients. An example is penicillin. Many patients develop diarrhea when they take penicillin, and they will call this an allergy to penicillin when actually it is just an unpleasant side effect. The same goes for codeine; patients will get nauseated with codeine, and label it an allergy when in fact it is just an unpleasant side effect. Why does this matter? Well, if you label yourself allergic to penicillin when you really aren't, you are limiting your physician's options for treating infections. If you mistakenly label yourself allergic to codeine, you are limiting your physician's options for treating your pain

◊　A list of past medical problems, and past surgeries; you can ask your physicians to each write up a list for you so you know it is accurate

◊　Your health care power of attorney and your POLST (Physician Orders for Life-Sustaining Treatment) document, if you have either one. More on these in the, "Legal Documents" chapter

◊　Copies of your insurance cards and driver's license

•　In the event that you must call an ambulance, have someone stand outside and flag them down. Ambulances can have trouble finding addresses, so this is a simple way to save time during an emergency.

There are so many challenges that people face when they land in the emergency room; it can make equipping and empowering yourself extremely difficult. Most commonly, an ER visit is an unexpected visit, so there is the stress of the medical condition itself. Medical emergencies can be a sudden medical crisis, or a worsening of a chronic condition. The physicians and nurses working there typically don't know the patient (though there are patients who are in the emergency room so often that ER staff will quietly refer to them as "frequent fliers"). It can be difficult to get your concerns conveyed because the staff is generally working at a fast pace to tend to multiple emergencies at one time. Some hospital emergency rooms might have upwards of 50-60 treatment beds with perhaps three doctors working! To add to it, patients and their loved ones often don't have a clear understanding of the patient's medical conditions, medications, or their rights.

On the subject of knowing your rights, you must be informed about EMTALA. EMTALA stands for the Emergency Medical Treatment and Active Labor Act. When you present to the emergency room, you have the right to:

- A medical screening exam to determine if a medical emergency condition exists

- Stabilization and treatment of emergencies, if possible

- Be transferred to a hospital that can treat you, if you cannot be stabilized in the facility you where you initially present on an emergent basis

This sounds pretty confusing, doesn't it? Let's look at a few examples to help clarify things. Let's say you are a Medicare Advantage patient, meaning that specific doctors and hospitals are contracted to see you. You can't just "show up" anywhere you wish; it is essentially a Medicare HMO plan. You are across town visiting a friend when you fall and you have a pain in your hip. You are brought to an emergency room not on your health plan.

Will they see you, even though they're not on your health plan? Yes, you have a right to a medical screening exam to determine if a medical emergency condition exists. In this case, you would be screened to rule out a broken hip or other injuries from your fall. If indeed you had broken your hip and required surgery, you would then have the right to stabilization and treatment of your broken hip. Now, just for example, let's say that the particular hospital you landed in doesn't have orthopedic surgeons on staff; you would have the right to be transferred to a hospital that can treat you.

To summarize the "labor" portion of the discussion of EMTALA, let's just say that if you're a pregnant woman in active labor, you're not going anywhere until that baby is delivered, unless the hospital doesn't offer obstetrical services. Transferring a pregnant woman who is in active labor is a big no-no!

When you present to the ER with an emergent condition, the confusion can be at a fever pitch. Heaven forbid, you're alone in this situation, but even if you aren't, your loved ones are trying to help you figure out so many things, it is also helpful to know who can do what to help you in an ER, so the next section will be of great value.

Who is working in the ER these days?

In the olden days, the emergency room was just that—a room staffed by totally inexperienced interns who had just graduated from medical school. There was little or nothing to be done for many medical emergencies because the technology had just not been developed. In 1979, the American Board of Emergency Medicine was created and emergency medicine became an official medical specialty, much like general surgeons or neurologists. Emergency medicine residency-trained physicians will staff most emergency departments in all but the most rural hospitals. In rural areas, where they may not be able to attract specialty physicians to the area, family practitioners or internal medicine specialists may still staff emergency rooms. Today's emergency medicine specialists complete medical school, followed by a year of internship, followed by three years of specialty training in emergency medicine. They spend time in the emergency department and in various areas of the hospital, such as the operating room, obstetrics/gynecology, pediatrics, and the general medical floors to gain an understanding of all aspects of medicine. ER docs have to know a lot, but they obviously can't know everything! Emergency medicine physicians specialize in recognizing and treating medical emergencies, mass casualties and disasters. They are definitely not there to replace your primary care physician.

It's important to realize that when you come to the emergency room, the emergency medicine physicians are only examining you for life-threatening emergencies. When patient X shows up complaining of chronic back pain for six years, he or she will probably not receive an extensive amount of testing. The ER doctor will rule out *life-threatening causes* of back pain; and if those aren't found, will likely send the patient on their way to follow up with their primary care physician as an outpatient. That is not bad care on the part of the physician, just the reality that the emergency room is only there to look for medical emergencies.

Who's on duty at the emergency room?

- ED physicians – ED stands for emergency department, it means the same as the emergency room. ED physicians are usually contracted by the hospital and are not typically hospital employees. What does this mean to you? You will receive a separate bill for their services, and in the case of allegations of medical malpractice, the hospital will quickly distinguish their liability from that of the ED physician.

- NPs or PAs – NP is a nurse practitioner, a registered nurse who has obtained additional training and certification to see patients on his or her own, with a physician co-signing their chart. A PA is a physician assistant, someone who has completed undergraduate college and two years of a graduate program designed to assist the physician in seeing patients. In some states, PA's can now see patients without a doctor co-signing; this was covered in a previous chapter. Be sure and ask the training of the person who is treating you; remember your patient's rights.

- RNs – registered nurses; we couldn't do without them.

- PCTs – Patient Care Technicians (or "Techs") Patient care technicians do so much for patients these days. They really are the "right arm" of registered nurses. They frequently put the patient in the room, help them change into a gown, hook up monitors, provide comfort. The only thing they really can't do is administer medications; that is the job of the registered nurse.

- Scribe – This is a person whose sole function is to take notes for the physician while they are speaking with you. They are a time-saver, and since they are only focused on taking notes, they can take more thorough notes. You may not even notice the scribe because they frequently stand in a back corner and don't ask any questions. EKG technician – This individual has completed training in obtaining and general interpretation of the EKG (electrocardiogram). Don't be shocked if the EKG technician is a male, and you are a female patient and they ask you to expose your chest. It is their job. If you're uncomfortable, feel free to ask for a nurse to be present while the EKG is being obtained.

- Respiratory Therapist – According to the Bureau of Labor (Bureau of Labor Statistics, 2015), respiratory therapists "Assess, treat and care for patients with breathing disorders. Assume primary responsibility for all respiratory care modalities, including the supervision of respiratory therapy technicians. Initiate and conduct therapeutic procedures; maintain patient records; and select, assemble, check, and operate equipment." If you require specialized breathing care, chances are, you'll be meeting a respiratory therapist.

- Orthopedic Technologist – Sometimes known as a cast technician, their professional organization, The National Organization of Orthopedic Technologists, says this (National Association of Orthopedic Technologists, 2013): "The OT is able to fit and adjust canes, crutches and walkers, as well as giving patient instruction on the use of these walking aids. Other important responsibilities of the OT are the ability to apply simple braces, prosthetics, perform minor adjustments and repairs, as well as fabricate splints for various conditions under the direction of the orthopedic surgeon." Please do not confuse OT orthopedic technologist, with an OT occupational therapist – they are totally different fields!

Other hospital staff that you may find helpful during your visit:

- Charge nurse – The emergency department "charge nurse" is in charge of the nurses during that particular shift. If you are having troubles with your nurse (or your physician, for that matter), it is wise to ask to speak to the charge nurse. Emergency Department Nurse Manager – This individual may or may not be working when you're in the emergency room. They are the manager of the ER. If you aren't getting anywhere with the charge nurse, the nurse manager is the next one "up the chain," so to speak.

- Hospital patient advocate – Please don't confuse a private, professional health care advocate with a hospital patient advocate. Hospital patient advocates are employees of the hospital, there to serve the best interests of the hospital. In the case of their interactions with patients, they are there to help the hospital to avoid getting sued. A hospital patient advocate can help with certain matters. One good example is pain control. If you feel your pain is not being adequately addressed in the ER, asking for the hospital patient advocate can help. For matters more medically complicated, you'll need a private professional advocate. Hospital patient advocates aren't going to look at every detail of your care; they are simply going to address the concerns that you voice. And they won't be able to spend unlimited amounts of time with you, either. Those roles would be left to a private advocate who only has your best interests at heart.

- Hospital social worker – Social workers in hospitals are experts at nursing home placement, and are quite knowledgeable about Medicare and Medicaid regulations.

- Hospital pastoral care – Enough cannot be said for pastoral care. These pastors will hold your hand through a crisis, pray with you, call family members, and sit with you during your most difficult times.

- Risk Management Department – This is a department of every hospital whose job it is to address issues of legal matters of the hospital. Whether it's avoiding a lawsuit, settling a lawsuit, or going to court, this is the department that handles it all. In some cases, private professional health care advocates have been known to contact the risk management department when things are going terribly wrong. While considered a dramatic and last-ditch step, it is incredible how much can change when risk management becomes involved. Could a patient contact the risk management department? Probably so, but just asking for their phone number may get you the improvements in your care that you need.

Teri Dreher

The Dance of the Emergency Department

Think of the dynamic ER environment much like an elaborate ballet performance, with doctors and staff changing at shift change, or when going to lunch, or when going on break. Add to this a litany of patients – some are just arriving, some are waiting to be seen, some are in the middle of testing, some are in the middle of treatment, some are staying to be admitted, and some are being discharged – all at the same time. If the ER is not managed well, it can feel exceptionally scary and chaotic to patients and their loved ones, and there can be many "cracks" in the system due to all of this constant change!

As you can imagine, the ER is a most unpredictable place. One minute it can be extremely quiet (though people who work in the ER are superstitious and will never use the "q" word for fear of an onslaught of patients), and the next moment there can be multiple ambulances arriving with all sorts of medical emergencies. There are also patients who arrive by private transportation, and they can be extremely ill as well. Many times in the ER, there are also patients who are admitted but waiting on a room in the hospital, so they are taking up a room in the emergency department and continuing to require care by the emergency department until a room is available for them. If you find yourself amongst the "waiting for a room upstairs" category in the ER, feel free to ask for a hospital bed to be brought in. You'll be much more comfortable, and will rest just a bit easier. Always keep in mind your rights as a patient!

One of the most important and potentially most "dangerous" parts of the emergency department for a patient is the triage area.

Think of triage registered nurses as the gatekeepers to the "Magic Kingdom" known as the emergency department. Typically, RNs are trained to work in the triage area. They are the ones who first perform an initial evaluation or "assessment" of the severity of your condition. Here is where the huge potential for troubles lies. The triage nurse decides upon the following: Is your problem "urgent," meaning that you (the patient) are so sick that you-need-a-room-right-now-no-matter-what kind of urgent. Is your problem emergent, meaning that you get the next room that becomes available, after the urgent folks are roomed? Or is your problem deemed non-emergent? If you are labeled non-emergent, it could be a very long wait for you in the ER, as you will be "bumped" in the queue by every urgent and emergent patient that arrives.

A 55-year-old woman was brought to a busy urban ER by her family because she was "acting crazy, not herself." The triage nurse performed their assessment on the patient, and deemed her "non-emergent," probably just another patient for the mental health department. The family, being very respectful and polite, tried to calm her as she was screaming uncontrollably and rolling on the floor in the emergency room waiting room. They had to trust that the triage nurse was correct in her assessment that this did not constitute a true emergency. By the time the security guards dragged this poor patient to a cart in the ER (she couldn't even walk at that point), it was quickly determined that this patient was suffering a massive heart attack. Sadly, her heart stopped and she could not be saved. Her "crazy" behavior was likely a lack of oxygen circulating to her brain from the massive heart attack. The triage nurse made a judgment call, and unfortunately it was not accurate in this case. What could've been done differently? Had the family been equipped by knowing their rights, they could have insisted that she be taken to the back and evaluated by a physician. There are too many stories of innocent errors in the triage area that have cost patients their lives, or delayed their care and worsened their outcome as a result. We are all human and can all make mistakes; our job as empowered patients and families is to have the courage to "buck the system" and speak up when things don't seem to be going as planned.

Tips to Equip: Your rights during your emergency department visit

You have the right to:

- Have access to emergency services (screening and stabilization) even if the hospital is out of your network and without financial penalty (EMTALA)

- Take part in treatment decisions. Just because you're a senior citizen or you are hard of hearing doesn't mean that you don't have a say in your own treatment

- Ask about pros and cons of treatment (even no treatment)

- Refuse any test or treatment (if you're deemed competent as discussed in the Patient Bill of Rights Chapter)

- Discharge yourself from the hospital, even against medical advice. However, if you sign yourself out "AMA" (against medical advice), your insurance company may stick you with the hospital bill

- Respect and consideration. Don't put up with surly nurses and rude physicians

- Privacy of health information. This one should go without saying, right? No one should be yelling your weight across the room to the other nurse

- Complaints and appeals. You have the right to complain, and you have the right to appeal without retribution.

- Treat everyone with kindness

- Ask for, remember (or write down) and use names of staff. Everyone loves to hear their name being used in a positive tone, and people tend to treat you better when they know that you know their name

- If the patient isn't able to speak for themselves, or doesn't feel up to it, have one family member "do the talking" for the entire family. If there's one thing that irks hospital staff and will turn them against you is repeatedly having to answer the same questions to different family members

- Take notes to recall what was said for review at a later time

Tips to Equip: If your ER visit isn't going well

- Ask for your nurse to come to the room and calmly discuss the issues. Remember, calm and rational win the fight. Angry, yelling and scary will just get you removed by hospital security.

- If your nurse isn't helpful, go "up the chain." Ask for the charge nurse. If he or she can't help, then ask for the emergency department nurse manager

- Have the ER physician summoned to the bedside. Ask direct questions in a calm and respectful tone. Avoid name-calling or threats to sue.

- When all else fails, ask for the phone number of the risk management department of the hospital and call. Oftentimes, just asking for the number will bring about sweeping changes in your care.

Tips to Equip: The discharge process if you're in agreement

Try and obtain copies of labs, X-rays, CT scans, EKGs, and any other test results to take with you. It makes follow-up with your physician so much easier and streamlined.

- If you will need follow-up, ask the ED physician to phone your physician before discharge to arrange it if they haven't already done so. When the ER doctor told Mrs. Smith to see a dermatologist in the next couple of days for her unexplained rash, she was shocked when she phoned the dermatologist and was told there was a six-month wait for an appointment! However, if a doctor phones another doctor and asks for that doctor to see you, you'll be seen the next day in most cases. If you call the same doctor on your own, chances are you're going to have to wait quite a bit longer, and in some cases months longer.

- Make sure you understand discharge meds and instructions. This cannot be stressed enough. In fact, Medicare will soon enact a new law requiring hospitals to educate you and your family about how to take care of you, the patient, at home.

Tips to Equip: *When you don't agree with discharge*

Without a doubt, this would be a great time to have a private, professional health care advocate. But assuming that you don't:

- Remain calm, state your concerns to the physician
- Take notes as the physician gives you their reasoning. Taking notes makes physicians really think about their words and actions. It demonstrates your concern for what they are saying, and is also "evidence" if something goes wrong
- Be firm in your convictions if you still can't agree
- If the physician is still planning discharge, go up the chain – charge nurse, emergency department nurse manager, and then risk management

Tips to Equip: *Admission to the hospital from the emergency department*

- If there are no rooms available in the hospital, and it looks like a long wait in the ED, request a hospital bed be brought in. You don't need to throw your back out sleeping on an ER cot when you're already ill with something else.
- Get clarification on drinking and eating restrictions. It's amazing how many patients starve while in the ER

waiting on a room, and can easily get a meal when they get to their room.

- If on Medicare, ask whether you are on observation status or a full admission. This is a very complicated issue, and the ER physician may not have a say in this. If you are on observation status, you are considered an outpatient, and Medicare will not pay for your medications in the hospital. In addition, if you are admitted under observation status and you need to go to a rehab facility, you are going to be stuck for the rehab facility bill. You cannot, under current Medicare laws, go to rehab without first spending three nights as an inpatient in a hospital (More on this in the Medicare chapter)

- If you're being admitted under "Observation" status, ask if you can bring in your usual medications from home. If they allow it, you can save a bundle of money on medications

Chapter 5

Dangers Lurking
In Every Hospital

In the past fifteen years, the issues of patient safety and medical error have been major areas of concern in hospitals throughout the country. In 2000, a landmark report was published that shook the medical establishment to its core: *To Err Is Human: Building a Safer Health System* (Linda T. Kohn, 2000). The report was written by The National Academy of Sciences, a group that describes themselves as "a private, nonprofit society of distinguished scholars charged with providing independent, objective advice to the nation on matters related to science and technology."

One of the authors of the report, Linda T. Kohn, further describes the organization's mission, "Upon the authority of the charter granted to it by the Congress in 1863, the Academy has a mandate that requires it to advise the federal government on scientific and technical matters." (Linda T. Kohn, 2000) The scholars in the committee noted that, as the health care system becomes more complex, there are more opportunities for medical error.

The National Academy of Sciences, in their *To Err Is Human* report, defined a few terms necessary to understand their findings:

- They defined "safety" from the patient's perspective, as *"freedom from accidental injury"*

- The phrase "adverse event" as *"injuries as a result of medical management."* Some adverse events are preventable, such as an infection the patient acquires as a result of improper hand washing by the medical staff

- The term "error" as *"the failure of a planned action to be completed as intended (i.e., error of execution), or the use of a wrong plan to achieve an aim (i.e., error of planning)"* (Linda T. Kohn, 2000)

Through examining hospital admissions data from 1997, the report concluded the following:

- Death caused by preventable adverse events occurred in at least 44,000 patients and possibly as many as 98,000 patients (Linda T. Kohn, 2000)

- Medical errors are the eighth leading cause of death in the United States; that is more deaths than from motor vehicle accidents or breast cancer

- The Academy estimated that the total national cost for preventable adverse events to be between $17 billion and $29 billion dollars

- Medication errors account for one out of 131 outpatient deaths (Linda T. Kohn, 2000)

- Medication errors account for one out of 854 inpatient deaths (Linda T. Kohn, 2000)

A 1997 study published in the medical journal Lancet reported, "In a study of 1,047 patients admitted to two intensive care units and one surgical ICU, 45.8 percent were identified as having had an adverse event, where adverse event was defined as "situations in which an inappropriate decision was made when, at the time, an appropriate alternative could have been chosen." (Andrews, Stocking, & Krizek, 1997)

In 2013, another study regarding medical error, "A New, Evidence-Based Estimate of Patient Harm Associated With Hospital Care" was published in the Journal of Patient Safety. (John T. James, 2014) The author conducted a literature review of four previous medical error studies, and found that the estimated 44,000 to 98,000 deaths per year due to medical errors numbers estimated in the, *To Err Is Human,* report to be a low estimate. He concluded that between 210,000 to 400,000 patients per year died due to medical error in hospitals. It's not surprising to those of us who work in hospitals. It's very similar to the fast food industry; those who work within know exactly what happens behind the scenes.

John James, the author of the 2013 study, concluded with this statement regarding the goal of reducing deaths due to medical error: "Fully engaging patients and their advocates during hospital care, systematically seeking the patients' voice in identifying harms, transparent accountability for harm, and intentional correction of root causes of harm will be necessary to accomplish this goal." (John T. James, 2014) We couldn't agree more, and we believe that private, professional health care advocates are a great way to meet the goal of reducing medical error and preventable deaths.

Personally, I believe these staggeringly horrible figures are still low. They are only the reported cases, and I know from observation within the medical system that there are wide variations in what actually happens versus what gets reported by the institutions themselves. Health care reimbursement for services is now very closely tied to a facility's safety statistics, and there is fierce competition to keep these numbers down. Hospital employees' salaries are often (at least indirectly) tied to their unit's rate of falls, infections, and medication errors.

About the incidence of medical error and the accuracy of reporting: you never know the real picture unless you work in the hospital setting every day. The problem is very real, and within each of us is hidden the best defensive tool available: our instincts. Every one of us knows what it feels like to sense when something is not right. Use your senses and instincts to tell you when something seems wrong, whenever you encounter a warning bell. That bell in our head is there to warn us of danger, and we should be alert and observant whenever we, or our families, are hospitalized. If something doesn't seem right, speak up and voice your concerns to hospital staff. Don't be rushed into signing consents for procedures you don't understand.

Most people view hospitals as very "safe" places—a respite when you are ill and need healing. In addition, most people think hospitals have got to be the cleanest place in town, right?

You hear about "hospital corners" on beds (the best-made beds around) and "hospital clean."

A Clean and Safe Environment

We briefly discussed your right to expect a clean and safe environment in the previous chapter. Now we will further drill down to exactly what is "safe" and what is "clean" as well as what you should be able to expect when you receive care in a medical facility where your health should be protected.

Most patients assume that hospitals are extremely clean places; this could not be further from the truth. Infections acquired while in the hospital are rampant, and can be lethal. Why? The germs (usually bacteria) found in hospitals have been exposed to many powerful antibiotics. While most germs are killed by the antibiotics, a few of the germs that have been exposed to the multitude of antibiotics survive because they have "figured out" or, in scientific terms, genetically mutated so that they are no longer killed by the antibiotics. These "superbugs" are known as antibiotic-resistant; they know how to resist being killed by antibiotics. Not only do they survive, they proceed to multiply. There are now bacteria for which science has no cure. We are seeing more and more of these "HAI's" also known as, hospital-acquired infections.

To illustrate this point, I will share the case of an elderly patient who had a worn-out hip joint; it needed to be replaced. The patient was in reasonably good health, and was cleared medically for the surgery. The patient would have done extremely well except that the new joint became infected, leaving the patient in a nursing home and on IV antibiotics for months, having to have the new joint surgically removed and replaced with another new joint, only to find out that the bacteria are now "colonized" in the joint and can never be eradicated.

The United States Centers for Disease Control and Prevention (the "CDC") reports, "On any given day, 1 in 25 hospitalized patients has at least one health care-associated infection." (Centers for Disease Control and Prevention, 2016) The CDC divides HAI's into one of three categories:

1) Surgery and catheter-related infections
2) Infections spread between patients
3) Improper antibiotic usage

Six common and often antibiotic-resistant bacteria cause many of these infections. Some bacteria, such as staphylococcus, live as a normal part of our skin, but when they enter a body cavity or an open wound, they cause an infection.

The culprit for the spread of many of these germs is very simple–the hands! Yes, the hands of the health care workers we entrust to restore our health. Improper hand cleansing is thought to be the culprit in many hospital-acquired infections.

Infection control

Infection is a major risk of entering a hospital; we can't mention it enough. Infection is defined as an invasion of the body by germs. When you cut yourself at home, the cut may get a little red but you put some antibiotic ointment on it with a bandage, and it gets better. Germs at home tend to be very easy to control because they haven't been exposed to massive amounts of antibiotics. Unfortunately, the germs found inside hospitals are the strongest and deadliest known to mankind. There are currently bacteria for which there is no effective antibiotic, and it is found inside hospitals. How would those bacteria reach you? Hospital personnel, either on themselves or on their equipment, would bring it to you.

Patients and their advocates need to be extremely vigilant and not be afraid to speak up when you see an activity that doesn't seem right to you. There is a big difference between "clean" and "sterile." Clean is just what we think of, washed. In a clean environment, bacteria are still present, but hopefully the numbers are low and hopefully they are just the normal bacteria that live on the surface of our skin. Taking blood pressure would be an example of a procedure where clean is all we need, not sterile since we are not breaking the surface of the skin. Gloves that come about 50 per box in a patient room are clean, but not sterile. They are fine for touching the outer surfaces of the skin, but not okay for procedures where skin will be broken. Sterile gloves can be identified by their being individually and double-wrapped.

Medication Errors

Unfortunately, medication errors and complications, as a result, are another very-significant risk in the hospital and outpatient setting. Becker's Hospital Review lists 10 safety issues in hospitals, many of which patients can't do much about, such as building maintenance and cyber security, but the issue of medication errors was significant on their list. (Becker's Hospital Review, 2016) Deaths due to medication errors are thought to account for 1 out of 894 hospital inpatient deaths and 1 out of 103 outpatient deaths. (Linda T. Kohn, 2000) Medications can be life saving, but harmful if used in the wrong circumstance or given to the wrong patient. Nurses are trained to administer medication while following the "Six Rights" of medication administration: the right patient, the right medication, the right amount (dose), given by the right route (think pill, IV, a shot or numerous other routes), the right time of day, supported by the right documentation.

Hospitals and pharmacies have policies and procedures in place to help reduce medication error, but errors still occur. One of the major issues is medication that sounds or looks similar. The Institute for Safe Medicine Practices publishes a list, which is formulated through medication and vaccine errors reported to them. (Institute for Safe Medicine Practices, 2015)

For medical personnel, the list is eye opening. Imagine that you are given Xanax (a sedating, anti-anxiety drug) instead of Zantac (for heartburn). This medication "sound-alike" is just one example of hundreds! We have heard first hand of a patient who was supposed to get a TB test (PPD) and was mistakenly given a tetanus shot (Td) instead. What can you, as a patient or a loved one, do to help avoid these sometimes-deadly errors?

Never Underestimate the Ramifications of Safety Measures

I got a call from a couple whose daughter had been transported to the emergency room after stopping a medication that managed her bipolar disorder. Their daughter was a professional, normally a very highly functional person, but bipolar patients often think they do not need their medication when they are feeling well. When they stop their meds, life can get very interesting very quickly. In this case, the patient had left her husband and small children and gone to a hotel room with a heroin addict whom she was convinced was the love of her life. She drank herself into an almost-unconscious state, and when her husband tracked her down, she threatened to kill herself. At that point, the patient was escorted to the local emergency room with the assistance of 911 and the EMTs.

She had been so violent that she needed to be put in restraints to keep her from doing harm to herself or others. Her alcohol level was over 300, which was very dangerous. After an hour or so she gave up fighting and convinced her nurses that she was fine, so her restraints were removed. She acted very rational and eventually convinced her husband that he could leave to go outside for a smoke. I'm not sure what happened next, but when the nurses came back to her ER cubicle, she was frantically rummaging around the drawers in her area, found partially used vials of controlled substances, and shoved them into her pockets. I listened to their story with eyes wide open, thinking, "Really?" Unlocked narcotics and sedation in drawers in the emergency room are such a violation of hospital safety codes on so many levels that I was truly aghast. I worked in a critical care area for years and I know the hoops we have to go through to sign out, to waste and document controlled substances. I could not believe such a violation of patient safety had occurred.

The parents of this patient had contracted my services because the ER staff had called the police, who had her taken to a local psychiatric facility and promised they would prosecute her upon her release. I'm not saying that the patient had made good choices that night, but the fact was that she was drunk and high out of her mind, and her rights to safety were violated by leaving her unattended shortly after her arrival at the ER with a near-lethal alcohol level and threat of suicide. She simply could not be trusted, and the staff had a responsibility to have a sitter with her at all times. I'm sure they were pretty freaked out when they saw what she had found in the drawers, and calling the police seemed like the logical next step.

It was probably a good thing for the hospital that the parents called me instead of a lawyer, because that ER could have been shut down in a heartbeat. They might have even encountered a huge lawsuit on the grounds of a patient's safety being violated. I like hospitals and I have empathy for the ER staff's position, so I thought I'd take a softer tactic, at first. I hate to see lawsuits against hospitals; the costs of multimillion-dollar lawsuits are, to me, one of the reasons why the cost of health care has skyrocketed over the years. I try to avoid lawyers at all costs. The day after I talked with the patient's parents, I made a friendly call to the hospital's risk manager. Every hospital has one; their job is to prevent lawsuits brought about by medical error. They have job security because every hospital in this country has their fair share of medical error; unfortunately, it's unavoidable, but it can be reduced.

Back to the phone conversation with the risk manager; I wanted to her to understand my role in this case. I wanted to convey that I understood very clearly that we had a major safety violation on our hands. My client's daughter was about to be arrested and likely lose her ability to work professionally due to the nature of her crime (she happened to be a nurse).

I said to the risk manager, "Help me understand what actually happened here, because I'm an ICU nurse and I know what we have to do to sign out and waste [dispose of] narcotics. I just cannot imagine a suicidal, drunk patient being left alone in a room where there were unlocked narcotics. I'm sure there are pieces of the story that we're unaware of. Perhaps you'd like to go talk to the manager of the ER and find out what really happened. I'd like to see us avoid going to court over this, but the patient's parents are pretty upset about their daughter getting arrested when she leaves the psychiatric ward. The patient was blacked out and doesn't remember a thing. Do you think we can try to work this out?"

We got off the phone on a respectful note and I waited for a return call, which came about 45 minutes later. The charges against the patient were completely dropped without incident. Her parents made certain she received psychiatric follow-up and a near calamity was avoided on the part of both parties. In this case, the patient's safety was compromised by, not only her state of mind and mental health, but also by the staff's negligence of proper protocol. My advocacy for the patient's ultimate safety (career, reputation, health) once her health was restored resulted in a positive outcome for all parties involved.

Tips to Equip: The difference between "clean" and "sterile"

- Clean is not good enough when we are talking about going deeper than the outer surface of the skin. Sterile procedure should be practiced when dealing with surgical sites, IV sites, drawing blood, and taking care of wounds. Sterile means free of living organisms. If a nurse tells you that she "can't draw blood wearing gloves," then ask for another nurse to draw the blood

- Taking blood pressure is a "clean" activity, not a sterile one since we are not going below the skin surface; staff should be wiping their stethoscope head with alcohol before it touches your skin

- Just wearing gloves is not enough; all staff should either wash their hands with soap and warm water or use hand sanitizer when they enter your room, before touching you, and before donning gloves. They should also wash or use sanitizer as they leave your room. Gloves can have microscopic holes, allowing bacteria from another patient to colonize on you, so the skin underneath needs to be clean

- To wash your wound, staff should use sterile gauze as the "washcloth" to cleanse your skin

- Health care workers ideally should not be wearing acrylic nails; all sorts of horrible bacteria are found underneath acrylic nails, and they cannot be scrubbed away. The CDC recommends that workers not wear acrylic nails when dealing with "high risk patients." The problem is that the CDC does not define a high-risk patient, but we personally feel that all hospitalized patients are at risk and acrylic nails should be avoided in all circumstances

- The CDC recommends that health care workers with natural nails keep them trimmed to ¼ inch in length, to reduce the numbers of bacteria under the nails (Centers for Disease Control and Prevention, 2016)

Patient Advocacy Matters

Tips to Equip: Avoid hospital-acquired infections

1. **K**eep your hands clean in the hospital. Here is a list from the CDC of when patients should wash their own hands: (Centers for Disease Control and Prevention, 2016)

    ◊ Before preparing or eating food

    ◊ Before touching your eyes, nose, or mouth

    ◊ Before and after changing wound dressings or bandages

    ◊ After using the restroom

    ◊ After blowing your nose, coughing, or sneezing

    ◊ After touching hospital surfaces such as bed rails, bedside tables, doorknobs, remote controls, or the phone

2. If using alcohol-based sanitizer, your health care worker should put the product on their hands, make sure all surfaces are covered, and rub their hands together until they're dry. This process should take around 20 seconds. (Centers for Disease Control and Prevention, 2016)

3. If the health care worker is washing using soap and water, they should first wet their hands, apply a hospital-approved soap, lather for at least 15 seconds while covering all surfaces of fingers and hands, rinse, dry hands with paper towel and use the paper towel to turn off the faucet (Centers for Disease Control and Prevention, 2016)

4.   The CDC has coined the phrase "speaking up for clean hands" (Centers for Disease Control and Prevention, 2016) and offers these tips:

◊   Ask your visitors to wash their hands; when they first arrive, ask them to wash; after they've been there for a while, ask them to wash their hands again (Think about them touching the furniture in your room, touching you, rides in the elevator, trips to the cafeteria and gift shop as sources of bacteria in a hospital)

◊   Make sure to keep your own hands washed

◊   Don't be afraid to ask your health care worker to wash their hands again if you didn't see them doing it as a clean environment is your right

◊   The CDC has a great line for talking to your health care workers about hand washing before performing any procedure. You can simply say, "I'm worried about germs spreading in the hospital. Will you please clean your hands once more before you start my treatment?" (Centers for Disease Control and Prevention, 2016)

5.   Urinary catheter infections are another common source of health care associated infections. (Centers for Disease Control and Prevention, 2016) While appropriate right after surgery, or if you're too ill to get out of bed to use the bathroom, each day that a catheter is left in increases your risk of infection. Ask your physician each day, "Do I still need this urine catheter?"

6.   The same goes for your IV. Intravenous catheters are sitting in your vein, creating a direct pipeline for bacteria to travel from your skin into your bloodstream. Ask your physician each day, "Do I still need this IV?" The worst they can say is, "yes, you still need it." If your IV is starting to look red, or is getting sore, please do speak up; it could mean that it's becoming infected (Centers for Disease Control and Prevention, 2016)

7.   If you're going to have surgery, ask your surgeon how he/she prevents infections during their procedures

Tips to Equip: Avoiding medication errors

- Don't distract your nurse with idle conversation when he or she is preparing to give you your medications or while they are discussing your medications with you while preparing for you to swallow them

- Know your pills, in every way possible; know their names, the reason you take them, their "strength" (frequently this is milligrams for pills), and the quantity of pills that you take in total. Josephine fortunately recognized that the quantity and appearance of the pills handed to her were not her usual. A caveat regarding recognizing your pills by sight is that you can't always go by a pill's appearance. Most facilities are using generic medications whenever possible now, and different manufacturers of the same medicine will produce pills of different shapes and colors than what you are accustomed. In Josephine's case, she had been receiving the same meds at the same facility for a couple of weeks, so she had grown accustomed to their appearance. This is obviously quite a bit more difficult in a hospital setting where your meds may be changing daily

- Have the nurse review every single pill with you before you swallow it. The nurse administers your meds off of a "medication order sheet," which is a personalized list of your meds and all their specifics. Follow along with the nurse as he or she is referring to your medication order sheet as they prepare to pass you your medications. Have them recite the name, the strength, the purpose of the medication, and for what time of day it is ordered. The pills should be in their original package and should be shown to you in the package so that you are certain that you are receiving the correct ones

Many people will read these recommendations and think that this is way beyond the scope of being a patient. It probably is, but won't you rest easier knowing that you are receiving the correct medications ordered for you? This is called advocating for *yourself*. If the thought of doing all of this double-checking causes you to have flashbacks of high school chemistry lab or the head-spinning days of algebra, then by all means consider hiring a private, professional health care advocate (PPHA) to help oversee your care in the hospital. PPHAs with a nursing or physician background have the education and experience to provide the oversight to help prevent medical errors and improve communication for hospitalized patients.

Tips to Equip: Protecting your safety while in the hospital

- You should leave jewelry and other valuables at home. For things that have been brought, there should be a way to lock your valuables so you are not a victim of theft

- Report any unusual behavior by your roommate (if you have one) or their visitors

- Alert staff to any spills you see on the floor

- There are also situations in which hospitals need to keep patients safe from themselves. Patients who are at-risk of harming themselves or others should be provided a 24/7 sitter to stay in their room and make sure they're safe. Here are a few common scenarios:

  ◊ When left alone, suicidal patients could seek out medications and/or objects left behind in exam rooms and harm themselves

  ◊ Patients with Alzheimer's or other forms of dementia can get very confused in the hospital and fall out of bed and suffer broken hips and head injuries

  ◊ Patients intoxicated by drugs or alcohol in the emergency room need to be continually observed, so that they do not wander out of the hospital and get hit by a car in the parking lot, or fall out of bed and hurt themselves or others; they are not in their right mind and their actions are unpredictable. It is the hospital's responsibility to keep them safe while they are under their care

Teri Dreher

◊ Weak and confused elderly patients are often
unaware of their limitations when they are ill, and
medications will also make them more unsteady on
their feet. If you notice an elderly person behaving
in an unsafe manner while in the hospital, please
alert the staff immediately. If you notice that your
family member appears weak, confused or dizzy
when standing, or they try to get out of bed on
their own, please alert the staff to institute "safety
precautions" or a "fall risk protocol" so that they are
more closely watched. If a patient is very confused,
a family member may want to act as a "sitter" to
watch their loved one at all times. If that is not
possible, the hospital may provide a "sitter" to sit at
the bedside and watch the patient at all times. Tell
staff that you are "concerned for their safety" and
they will have to do something to provide for an
extra layer of protection. You know your family
member better than anyone, after all

Section IV

Senior Citizens

I might refer to this chapter as my favorite, within this book, as the elderly hold a special place in my heart. We see a lot of senior orphans in our practice, and I continue to grow increasingly concerned for their safety. They are also the segment of the population who worry me the most–especially those with no family available to help them ask the right questions, tell their history or provide the correct list of medications and allergies when they need help. Unfortunately, this population is growing, day-by-day, in our society as baby boomers age, spouses die, children live on the other side of the country and physical challenges grow every year.

Some call them "senior orphans" or "solo-agers," but at the very least, they are vulnerable in today's fast-paced world of health care. These seniors or adults with disabilities need a friend to come alongside and help them navigate the short-term as well as the long-term crises they encounter. If they have children who don't live nearby, oftentimes, the children do not even realize how much their parents are struggling when they only talk over the phone and/or visit once or twice a year.

The elderly are particularly vulnerable to medical error when they enter into hospitals. Part of the reason why is because when they feel poorly, they don't eat and physical therapy is not initiated early enough. They get weak easily and are sensitive to new medications that may cause confusion, falls, complications of bed rest and hospital acquired infections. Their immune systems are weaker to begin with and they catch infections easily when they are around more germs.

Many times we have seen unsuspecting cases of someone's mother going into the hospital for a pelvic fracture that leads to pain, which leads to immobility and poor appetite. The downward spiral is inevitable as the immobility often leads to bedsores, pneumonia and sleep deprivation. Sleep deprivation leads to confusion, which leads to falls and ultimately, fractures. It is heartbreaking for families who have an implicit trust that, when they send grandma to the hospital for healing, the hospitalization actually results in further harm being done.

An important chapter in this section focuses on, "Options for Senior Living," because the reality is that, at some point, the family may have to decide whether or not their parents are safe to continue living independently. That conversation alone can stir up so many emotions because there are many things to consider. Will the parents come and live with their children? Are they safe to live alone? Is assisted living an option? What about their financial situation? Do they need a caregiver?

This where a PPHA can become an invaluable asset, not just to the person who needs the care, but to provide an immense sense of relief to the family who most likely are part of the sandwich generation we discussed earlier. They have no idea how to navigate this new world of taking care of mom and/or dad as well as their children and spouse, while possibly living half a country away from the parents.

It's a lot to consider, so I just hope the information presented here provides you with peace of mind, along with equipping you with the set of tools you need to help you make decisions that are informed and best for your unique situation.

Chapter 6

The Value of a Healthy Relationship with Your Doctor

Your Relationship with Your PCP Holds the Key to Your Ultimate Well-Being

Finding a primary care physician in today's health care world is more complicated than it used to be. Gone are the Marcus Welby medical care scenarios of the past, where it was just fine to have a family doctor *and* he knew your history by heart. You could also count on seeing his familiar face wherever you needed to be seen: office, home, hospital, or ER.

Many patients wonder whether they should look for a family practice physician, or an internal medicine physician. Knowing the difference between the two can help you decide. A family medicine physician is a physician who has undergone a three-year family medicine residency, learning how to treat "everyone" from newborns to the elderly. In theory, a family medicine physician sounds good as he can "steer the boat," if you will. He can become familiar with your entire family; you will see the same physician as your children and your spouse; he will get to know your family history; and that can possibly aid in his treatment of you. However, the practical problem with this specialty is, depending on your needs, there is realistically, no way any physician can learn detailed care of every age group in just three years. But if you enjoy fairly good health, or if you want to be able to see the same doctor as your children, then a family medicine physician can be a great choice.

If your health needs are more complex (either due to a chronic, complex illness or aging), you may want to consider an internal medicine specialist. Internal medicine specialists are never trained in treating children, so they are considered a physician for adults. They spend three years in residency learning only adult care. Many medical specialists, such as geriatricians, hematologist/oncologists, cardiologists and pulmonologists, first complete an internal medicine training, so it is the basis for a great deal of adult medicine.

Finding a Good Physician

Many people ask us how to find a good physician. The truth is, it can be tricky. Internet sites like <u>healthgrades.com</u> or <u>zocdoc.com</u> are fine to search for the basics. You will usually be able to find the physician's contact information, educational background, board certifications, and possibly malpractice and sanction history at these sites. You will frequently find patient reviews there as well. Keep in mind, however, that physician recommendations are not always accurate. Disgruntled patients sometimes make completely false accusations, and some sites may have dozens of glowing recommendations posted by the office's marketing department.

Try to get a recommendation from nurses or doctors, or ask to whom they would send their own family members. That is usually a pretty good endorsement. If you happen to find a physician on the internet, or a friend tells you about their physician, ask a nurse that you know (be sure you make it clear that this conversation is "between you and him/her") which internist or family medicine specialist on staff at that hospital would she choose for her family to see. You probably won't get far if you word the question in other ways, such as "What do you think of Doctor X?" Asking whom they would bring their family member to see will yield an honest and positive response, and you're not asking the nurse to say anything bad about any physician. You can do something similar if searching for a specialist: Call the hospital's physician referral hotline and ask which physician they would recommend to a family member. Then do your homework. I have found that if doctors I know who work in hospitals will tell me who they send their own family members to, that is the best compliment of all.

Too many medications aren't necessarily a good thing

We had a client whose son contacted us because his mother was becoming increasingly forgetful and dizzy at home. Upon review of her medications, we saw that she had been prescribed a sleeping pill that has dangerous side effects, particularly in elderly women. When she told her doctor that she was having problems during the daytime with restlessness and dizziness, he prescribed a second medication for anxiety that compounded her problems. Her doctor suggested that she might be developing Alzheimer's when, in fact, she was being overmedicated. Once she got a new doctor and was weaned off the medications, her symptoms disappeared and her son exclaimed, "I have my mother back again!"

Fortunately this frail, elderly woman did not have any falls or accidents related to the dizziness she experienced as a result of her two psychotropic medications, but many seniors do have tragic consequences of being overmedicated. Unfortunately, patients often expect to receive a prescription for any problems they are experiencing when they go to a doctor. It is wise to remember that all medications have side effects, and the more one is on, the higher the risk of interactions that may lead to harm, injury, or even worse.

We recently got a call about a 92-year-old woman whose son was concerned about his mother's safety after she had sustained a fall, breaking three ribs. When we met her, we saw that this tiny woman was on 14 medications, five of which had side effects of vertigo. Older adults are more sensitive to medications, so they usually require lower doses than someone younger. One of the medications she was on was a powerful diuretic at a dose that a 40-year-old man would take. We were able to go to our client's doctor appointment with her the following week, which resulted in several medications being discontinued or lowered. Once the doctor saw on paper how many medications our client was on, it was easy to see how many of them could cause the dizziness that had led to her fall. Some of them had also likely contributed to a gradual weight loss over the past six months as well. To support her continued and optimal health, a nutritionist that we now work with has been able to put her on a high-nutrition diet that her caregivers will help her follow. Even though our client is 92-years-old, her vision of quality of life includes living in her own apartment with the right support and we are helping her do that.

Tips to Equip: Before you make your first appointment with a new doctor, ask:

- Will I see the same person for primary care each time I come to the office?

- What happens when I go to the hospital?

- Does the doctor accept Medicare and/or my insurance?

- How long does it typically take to get an appointment if I am sick?

- Can you tell me if the doctor has experience treating (my specific ailment)?

- What hospitals does the doctor have admitting privileges at?

- What is the office appointment cancellation policy?

- Is there a policy for phone calls after hours? (Some offices will charge for after-hours phone calls.)

When you have an appointment with your new physician, it is best if you can bring a list of your current medications (prescription and over the counter), supplements, and vitamins that you're taking. Don't forget to write down any medications or foods that you're allergic to (some vaccinations, for example, are egg-based, so food allergies can still be important). Inform your new medical team of any past medical problems you've had, current medical problems and past surgeries. Be upfront about other physicians that you're still seeing as well. It is important for physicians to communicate with each other. Having the information written down before you arrive is valuable as it is easy to forget things when you're nervous.

Plan to arrive to your appointment about 15-minutes early to relax a bit (makes for better blood pressure readings) and fill out new patient forms. Be sure to introduce yourself to the staff and try and learn their names too. It is very helpful when you have to communicate over the phone with them in the future; this helps them have a sense of who you are.

We discussed many of the following in the, *Patient Bill of Rights* chapter, but from the very beginning of your relationship is when your rights come into play, not just when there might be a problem. When you meet a new physician, try and stay aware of how you're feeling about him or her. Is he or she making eye contact? Are they listening to my concerns, or cutting me off as I'm speaking? Do they seem rushed? Are my questions being answered to my satisfaction? Are my patient's rights being respected? Am I being treated with respect and consideration? Do I have a role in discussing treatment options? If I disagree, am I being treated with respect? Is the physician more focused on the computer than on me as a person?

Medications: The Good, The Bad and The Ugly

Very few will argue that medications have the potential to prevent, modify, and cure disease as well as improve the length and qualify of life. But are there down sides to these medications? To quote an old Western movie title, we need to consider the good, the bad and the ugly when contemplating whether or not to take a medication.

We've already discussed medication errors in the previous chapter. Let's examine some recent news reports regarding a very commonly used class of heartburn/gastroesophageal reflux disease (GERD) medications that physicians refer to as proton pump inhibitors (PPIs). We mere mortals know these meds by common brand names such as Nexium, Prilosec, and Prevacid, or generics such as omeprazole or esomeprazole, in addition to the plethora of other names used to reference them. Here's the *good*: PPIs are extremely effective for heartburn/acid reflux. They have improved the quality of life and prevented as well as cured serious gastrointestinal health problems for many, many people. Over the years, they have also been thought of as safe, so they are widely used. Their effectiveness and popularity are demonstrated by the many different PPIs available, both by prescription and over the counter.

Now here's the *bad* part: A **recent medical study** published in the Journal of the American Medical Association, *JAMA,* found an association between the use of PPIs and chronic kidney disease. Another recent study, published in the medical journal *JAMA Neurology*, reports a statistical association between the use of PPI medications with a 1.4 fold increased risk for the development of dementia. We do need to make one thing clear here, and that is that an "association" *does not prove* that proton pump inhibitors *cause* dementia or chronic kidney disease; only that there is a statistical association between their use and an increased risk for the development of these diseases. The reason for these associations is not understood, and to study cause-and-effect, randomized clinical trials will need to be performed. So while it's best to pay attention to news reports regarding medications, you need to keep in mind the potential problems and limitations of medical research and keep an open dialogue going with your physician regarding your medications. Also, keep in mind that acid in the stomach breaks down proteins properly, so when you take that acid away, you may have other digestive complaints. Some have noticed that simply losing 20 pounds or sleeping with your head up at night and not eating within three hours of going to bed can alleviate symptoms entirely.

Here's the ***really ugly*** part: Untreated medical conditions can lead to other, more serious health problems, disability and early death, things perhaps much worse than the possible negative effects of a medication. So, not treating conditions is most often not a good option. Even heartburn or GERD can have some very serious complications, and there is no disputing that PPIs have improved quality of life as well as saved lives and prevented and treated some serious health problems for many people. While there are alternative treatments available for GERD, they may not be right for your particular circumstances, and you should not abruptly stop your PPI (or any other prescribed medication, for that matter) without first consulting your physician.

The Rising Costs of Medication
Consumers are paying more for their medications, and they are not happy about it. To understand the "why" of any price increases in health care today, one has to understand the national impact that the Affordable Care Act has had on providers, insurers and pharmaceutical companies. To be simplistic, think of a balance scale or a seesaw on a playground. When reimbursement rates

by Medicare or private insurers decrease, prices have to come up to balance out the bottom line. Pharmaceutical companies are using many strategies today to preserve their profit margin; and consumers are paying more out-of-pocket costs for most health care-related expenses, including prescriptions.

A long list of medications isn't necessarily a good thing
"Polypharmacy" is a new term for something many people already know far too well. Among seniors today, 44 percent of men and 57 percent of women over 65 take five or more medications every week. Twelve percent of seniors take over 10 medications weekly. (American Geriatric Society)

When people take too many medications, often prescribed by different health care practitioners who are not communicating with each other, dangerous side effects and interactions can occur and go unnoticed until a crisis happens. It is important to always keep a complete list of medications (including vitamins, supplements, and OTC meds) with you at all times, so that all health care providers have correct information should you suddenly need hospitalization.

Taking medications is an even more serious issue for older adults. As we age, our kidneys and liver do not break down medications as well, and a "normal" dose of a medication can quickly become toxic. Other times, medications just don't work well, or they give older people terrible side effects, possibly leaving them sicker than before they took the drug.

In 2012, the American Geriatric Society updated their Beers Criteria for Potentially Inappropriate Medication Use in Older Adults. (American Geriatric Society) This is an important document for seniors, as it lists medications that should potentially be avoided in older adults due to extreme side effects or increased risks of complications. Many of the medications that made it onto the list of, "Beers Criteria List of Potentially Inappropriate Medications" for use in older adults cause symptoms such as confusion, hallucinations, sleepiness, blurred vision, difficulty urinating, dry mouth and constipation.

As you can imagine, if an older adult takes a medicine that makes them dizzy, they risk falling and breaking a hip or hitting their head, or having huge changes in their thinking abilities due to certain medications. Family members might believe their loved one is developing Alzheimer's disease when in reality, the changes in thinking they're seeing may just be due to medications.

If you have access to a computer, go to www.americangeriatrics.org and search Beers Criteria and you can view the Beers Criteria medication list for yourself.

Tips to Equip: When your doctor gives you new medication, ask about:

- The reason you are recommending this medication
- The side effects (Side effects are bothersome things that may occur with a medication. Usually not life threatening, but annoying; for example, drowsiness with Benadryl, or diarrhea with antibiotics)
- The dangers to taking this medication (Physicians refer to these dangers as adverse effects)
- Possible interaction with of my other medications

- Alternatives to taking this particular medication

- What could happen if I don't treat this condition with medication

Tips to Equip: Questions to regularly ask about your medications

- Do I still need this medication?

- Have there been any reports I need to know about regarding the safety or effectiveness of this medication?

- Are there any lifestyle modifications I can make to reduce or eliminate my reliance on this medication?

Tips to Equip: Keeping prescription costs down:

- Always to request a generic equivalent if your physician agrees (There are a few brand-name medications that are clearly superior to generic, but for the most part, a medication is a chemical component that is the same no matter what the fancy name or packaging)

- While you are in the doctor's office getting that new prescription, ask for samples. (Pharmaceutical reps give away billions of dollars a year to doctors at their offices in an effort to convince them of the superiority of their drug. Most of the time doctors forget about this option, and so they have closets full of samples, which will go to waste if they are not given away)

- A third option once you know you will be on the medication long-term is to request a 90-day prescription with three refills so you can get it from a mail-order pharmacy at deeply discounted costs

- Finally, don't forget to take advantage of drug discount cards and do cost comparison on sites like **goodrx.com**, **WeRx.org**, and **LowestMed.com**. **NeedyMeds.org** has a huge database of medications that may be subsidized for low-income people or those without insurance

- If you want to try to purchase your prescriptions online, make certain any online pharmacy has the VIPPS (Verified Internet Pharmacy Practice Sites) seal on the website to make sure you avoid Internet scams

Tips to Equip: Managing the side-effects of medications

1. Keep a list of all of your prescriptions, over the counter medications, vitamins, and supplements that you take, along with their strength and how often you take them. Bring this list to every physician at every appointment

2. Ask your doctor if any of your medications are known to have side effects. Check the American Geriatric Society's Beers Criteria, and if any of your medications are on the list, ask your physician about whether that drug is right for you. To quote the American Geriatric Society, "Keep in mind that if a drug you take is on one of the lists in the *AGS Beers Criteria*, this does not necessarily mean that it poses greater risks than benefits *for you*. The way *you* respond to a medication or medications can differ from the way other people respond to it. This is

why the experts who updated the criteria use the phrase
"*potentially* inappropriate." While the drugs on the lists
may cause side effects in some older adults, they won't
necessarily cause these problems in *all* older people."
(American Geriatric Society)

3. Never discontinue taking a medication on your
    own without consulting your doctor. Discontinuing
    some medicines suddenly can cause death or serious
    complications. An empowered, educated and equipped
    patient is a smart patient who doesn't try to practice
    medicine without a license

Chapter 7
Senior Orphans And Elder Abuse

Senior Orphans

We see a growing problem with a particular group of seniors who fall through the cracks of modern health care more than others: senior orphans.

What is a senior orphan? Simply put, it is a person over 65 who falls into one of three categories: (1) no family left; (2) family who has no regular contact with the isolated senior (i.e. dysfunctional families or those who live in other parts of the country); or (3) family who is taking advantage of the senior financially, depleting funds that may be needed for long-term care.

One of the sad facts of our society today is that there is a growing concern among some of us who work in the senior care industry with the issue of elder financial abuse. Not only are seniors being taken advantage of by scam artists and "helpful" neighbors who weave their way into the vulnerable person's life and gain access to bank accounts and retirement funds; I have noticed that many times, the perpetrator is most often a family member.

Teri Dreher

We regularly encounter sons and daughters who are reticent to approve needed expenses for long-term care of their parents because they are experiencing financial stresses themselves. They are afraid that there will be no inheritance left for them if Mom or Dad gets transferred to an assisted-living facility or quality, skilled nursing facility. The reality is that higher-quality nursing homes rarely admit people when their resources are almost depleted and they are in the process of applying for Medicaid. The better skilled nursing facilities require at least one year of private pay from patients before they transition to Medicaid payments for skilled care.

Elder abuse can also be something as simple as giving grandchildren a car when they are also living on limited means. Seniors love their grandchildren and want to see them enjoy gifts prior to their passing. When family members receive financial "gifts" from their parent's or grandparent's in the latter part of their lives, it may actually disqualify the senior from receiving Medicaid if they run through their savings and need to receive Medicaid benefits for long-term care expenses (more about this in the *Intricacies of Medicare* chapter). They justify the gift by telling themselves that the "black sheep" grandchild just needs a bit of help to get back on their feet and they anticipate dying before long anyway, so they just give it away now, so they can enjoy giving.

Running out of money before they die also happens to be one of the biggest concerns or fears faced by the aging population– even more so, if they have no family to depend on. The good news is there is help available. A wise financial planner and elder law or estate-planning attorney can often alleviate those fears,

164

help seniors protect their assets and avoid costly financial errors. There are many new and creative ways to help people protect their assets and plan wisely for long-term care needs. They can also help by offering solutions for what happens if they should run out of money, yet still look forward to many years of life to live and health care to receive.

The important thing to remember is that there are options, and no one needs to worry about being put on the street once their money runs out. This is also an important reason to find a "driver" to help your family navigate the course wisely. The fear of the unknown can be paralyzing, but I promise you this: it is always better to know your options versus being left in the dark and suffering needlessly due to worrying.

Caroline's Story

Earlier this year, I received a call from an attorney in another state who referred a woman to me that was reporting that she was being held in a nursing home against her will, and bad things were happening to her every day. To be honest, I first suspected that the woman may have dementia or a mental illness, but I decided to go check it out myself, just in case, and report back to the attorney on my findings.

When I went to the nursing home, the front desk personnel were very friendly, and the main floor looked older, but fairly clean, so I took the elevator upstairs and walked into a crowded nursing station area. Flanked on one side of the hall, there were several very pathetic-looking seniors tied into wheelchairs, crying and yelling, wailing and begging for help, while staff members stood by socializing in the nurses' station. They were ignoring the patients, who were obviously in advanced stages of dementia or perhaps even mentally ill. I proceeded to the patient in question's room, anxious to see what I might find there.

Caroline, a petite woman of 76, sat in her bed waiting for me, and had a mask over her face and mouth. She was one of four patients in the room, and had been transferred to a four-bed ward after her 100-days of Medicare had run out. The other patients in the room wore blank stares, either curled up in a corner, trembling, or leaning over the side of the wheelchair they were strapped into. Caroline seemed somewhat anxious and began to tell me her story, which I believe to be true.

Thirty years ago, her husband left her and her four young children, divorcing her for a new woman he had met, and offering little support after the divorce, though he was a well-off businessman. He was foreign-born and she had met him when she traveled to the Middle East. His ethnic background was very patriarchal—women had few rights and were not respected as Americans generally have come to expect. Caroline was an American and refused to dwell on her unfortunate circumstances, but rather made the best of things and moved on. She put herself through school, eventually earning a real estate license. She also started a home design and real estate company, and her children enjoyed the advantage of higher education. All four children were now successful in their various careers.

Both the father and oldest son were reported to be alcoholics and philanderers, and as her children grew up, they gravitated more toward their father. They rarely visited their mother, and she was heartbroken. The oldest son and his wife lived in Canada and had a two-year old son, whom Caroline had not yet seen. When I met Caroline, she had been in three low-rent-type nursing homes in the past six months. She had one broken, dislocated wrist that had needed surgery for several months. She had not seen a doctor since arriving at the present nursing home two months earlier. Doctor appointments, MRI scans, and medicines had been canceled at the last moment on multiple occasions. She could not sleep for the loud wailing and crying of other patients in the halls every night. She often missed meals, or they arrived late and cold. The nurses gave her incorrect medications every day, or refused to give her meds that she had relied on for years to prevent recurrence of cancer that she had been treated for successfully years ago. She was distraught and desperate to leave the nursing home to return home with 24-hour caregivers, which she could afford since she owned several large properties in a prestigious suburb of Indiana.

When I asked her how she had come to be a nursing home patient, her story became even more troubling. She suffered from several chronic medical conditions; and six months earlier she had gone to the hospital to undergo a CAT scan. Although she had told the tech that she was allergic to the dye used and the sedative they wanted to give her, they gave it to her anyway and she suffered an anaphylactic reaction to the medication, resulting in a cardiopulmonary arrest. She was put on life support, transferred to a major medical center, and woke up a week later. While she was incapacitated (even though she had named her oldest son her health care power of attorney years earlier) she found out that her son had hired a shark of an attorney to file a motion for an emergency guardianship order. This effectively took away all her rights to manage her own affairs or even pay her own bills. Her assets were frozen and her mortgage, taxes, licenses, and utilities were all unpaid and she was in danger of losing her properties.

At this point, I could not even contract with this client since she essentially had no legal rights, and was prevented by the court from even having access to her own bank account.

After I left Caroline's room that day, my mind raced. How could I help her, since she could not even hire me? I contacted the attorneys who told me there was nothing they could do. I asked for suggestions. One told me to contact her guardian ad litem, an attorney appointed by the court to protect her rights and advocate for her. He told me to report her present conditions to the guardian's attorney, who was the eldest son who lived in Canada.

When I called this man and told him that I was a nurse advocate and wanted to report that she was a victim of medical negligence and wanted the guardianship removed since she was clearly mentally competent, he started yelling at me and accusing me of HIPAA violations. He told me in no uncertain terms to stay away from her and to have no further contact with her. I got off the phone after politely asking him to please tell her son that she was in a terrible situation and needed to get into a better place soon. The attorney sounded very unconcerned for the patient's dire straits. I was stunned. What was going on here?

I decided to go to her next court hearing to see what I could learn. Before I went, I sought counsel from one of the best guardianship/mental health attorneys in Chicago. He told me what typically happened at hearings on guardianship matters and advised me to be a very quiet fly on the wall if I were to observe the open court hearing. What I saw in court confirmed my suspicions that Caroline was right: her sons likely did not have her financial best interests in mind. Her son's attorney portrayed the family as very devoted and concerned for her welfare, but asked permission to sell one of her properties to pay for her long-term care needs. Children who had visited their mother once in the previous six months were portrayed as devoted and concerned for her best interests.

I went home wondering what was true. Was Caroline really being imprisoned against her will, by sons who wanted full access to her finances, hoping that she would die in the low-quality nursing home so that they would inherit the $1,750,000 that she was worth? Why would professional children raised by a single mother not visit her, yell at her on the phone and threaten to never talk to her again if she did not go along with the guardianship? If Caroline is right, this is one of the saddest cases of family betrayal that I have ever seen.

One positive thing that came out of the court hearing was that Caroline was permitted to request an attorney of her own choosing; she asked for my friend who was one of the top attorneys in Chicago.

I could tell that everyone in the room was shocked at her bold request, and they all looked at each other and kindly told Caroline that, "in case he cannot accept your case, is it okay if we choose another for you?" She told the judge that this would be okay.

Imagine the shock when my friend's partner accepted the case a few minutes later outside the courtroom.

This story is a great example to all of us of the plight of seniors with dysfunctional families who rob them blind and put on a smiley face for the courts, as families who are only concerned for the patient's welfare. While there are many cases when guardianship must be pursued when patients leave no instructions to family members on their wishes through a power of attorney for health care document, there are always people out there who will take advantage of their parents when they are at their weakest and most vulnerable.

This case has kept me up at night, praying and hoping to find ways to help this poor woman. I will admit that I have refused to heed the advice of her son's attorney. I still visit her, talk to her daily on the phone and try to help on the sidelines until the day she is released from her captivity and is once again able to be captain of her own ship. I am hoping that day comes soon. I am beginning to understand why our state needs a department of elder abuse and adult protective services. Unfortunately, they are some of the most overworked and under appreciated heroes of our state government.

Not all cases that look like this actually turn out to be actual cases of elder abuse and neglect, however. I respect and admire attorneys who work in the industry and can weed out truth from fiction. On more than one occasion, I have been wrong about a sad story that turned out to be a mentally unbalanced patient who was weaving a tall tale. In this business, often truth is stranger than fiction. In the vast majority of cases, the U.S. justice system works, though more slowly than some of us wish it would.

Tips to Equip: Prepare for the possibility that you may become incapacitated

1. Take the time and make the investment in having legal papers drawn up to enforce your wishes. It's not enough to write down your wishes and get it notarized. There must be legally binding documents in place. Only a legal expert in this field will know how to ensure your wishes are respected if you are no longer able to advocate on your own behalf.

2. As you have your legal documents drawn up, be sure to differentiate the assignment for your health care and your finances (more on this in the *Documents and Insurance* chapter).

3. Periodically review the documents you have drawn up to ensure they reflect your current wishes and not the wishes you had 10 years ago. Those wishes may not reflect the existence of your designee, nor your current relationship.

Chapter 8

Options For Senior Living

Options for Safer Independent Senior Living, Assisted Living, Memory Care, and Nursing Homes

In recent years, the number of high-quality, skilled nursing facilities (SNFs or nursing homes) has dwindled due to the reduction in reimbursement rates by Medicare to SNFs. The ones who are most in demand often have long waiting lists. For Medicaid patients, the options are even fewer. It is a tangled web out there today, and my focus is usually to keep our senior clients out of hospitals and nursing homes as much as possible. A little prevention and careful attention to small details can make a big difference for seniors. The food at SNFs is not always what individuals want to eat, and their rates of infection can be quite high, so we like to explore all options before making this decision with our clients. With a private health advocate on their team, some patients can remain in their home with nursing care, enjoying the comforts of their own home and food that they enjoy eating. For those who are unable to afford the private pay of having a PPHA and a high-quality home care company that the care manager nurse oversees, we refer them to community organizations that can make referrals.

The cost of care in assisted living and skilled nursing facilities is inexpensive, and Medicare doesn't pay for long-term care in assisted-living or SNFs. The only time Medicare pays for SNF care is after a hospitalization, and it is only for a maximum of 100-days. According to a 2011 survey by Met Life, the national average cost for basic services in an assisted living facility is $41,724 a year, and for a nursing home it's $78,110 for a semi-private room and $87,235 for a private room. (Met Life Market Institute, 2011)

We have discussed the growing numbers of members of the Sandwich generation in a previous chapter, so we are already aware that many of us will find ourselves, at some point, in the heartbreaking scenario of suggesting or encouraging our parent(s) to move to a safer place to live. Investing in your parent's care and support as they age is never a bad idea. The reasons that it may no longer be safe to live alone are numerous, but frequently, the reasons are related to memory issues. Most people, when hearing the words memory loss, immediately think of Alzheimer's disease. While Alzheimer's disease is the most common type of dementia, it is not the only one. The memory loss may also be normal aging (what many call "senior moments," such as forgetting someone's name), MCI (mild cognitive impairment), vascular dementia, a thyroid condition, a head injury, or a medication side effect that is causing the change in cognition. To get a definitive reason for the decline, the patient will need to see a neurologist for testing. It may not be an easy task to get the person with cognitive decline to a neurologist; it is a very delicate issue, and it may take time to convince them to even get any testing done because they may be in denial of how serious the memory issues have become. It's also possible that they are (understandably) totally frightened at the possibility of Alzheimer's disease. One suggestion is to couch the issue of the visit to the neurologist around the fact that there are many treatable reasons for memory loss. Explaining that the only way to find those treatable causes is to go see the physician and be evaluated just may help, depending on the circumstances. Regardless of the reason for the memory loss, the focus still needs to remain around the issue of safety.

Many families are often afraid to broach the subject of mental impairment as they watch their parents age. Confronting a loved one about their memory issues often brings up feelings of betrayal, denial, anger and embarrassment for the person with the memory loss, and guilt for the adult children or spouse. Let's face it—it would be difficult to admit to your loved ones that you have lost your ability to safely live alone. Memory loss often happens slowly and people tend to hide the signs.

Unless you spend a significant amount of time with your parents or grandparents, it can be months or even years before the harsh reality hits. Seniors are often very resistant to moving, feeling that going into a senior living community constitutes a surrender of one's independence and dignity, and signifies the "end of the road." The reality is that many assisted and independent living communities are far from depressing. They have all the amenities of home, and many conveniences that make life much easier and safer for seniors. Sadly, the decision to delay a move can be a dangerous one. Remember the old adage, "If you fail to plan, you plan to fail." It is tragic when an accident or other medical calamity makes the decision an urgent and even more stressful one.

If you notice that the senior in your life is becoming more and more forgetful, the best thing to do is have a family meeting without your senior loved one before there is a crisis. The purpose of the meeting is to plan a unified and loving approach to the discussion of moving. If there is a unified consensus and a willingness to help all around, the move will be much easier, with no hurt feelings on anyone's part. The message should be a clear and loving one: "Mom, we love you too much to see you live alone any longer. If you fall, or if anything dangerous happens, we would be heartbroken. We see how you are struggling (give examples here), and we all agree that the time has come to choose a better living situation."

After you and the rest of the family present the idea of moving, let the parent or couple speak and ask as many questions as possible. It is important that they know that they are respected and are being heard. Oftentimes, they will admit that they need help. Sometimes, they won't be ready to have the conversation and will react with anger. If that should happen, save it for another day, and another gentle conversation.

The reason for resistance to moving may be the daunting task of moving itself. Moving is overwhelming to most of us, but especially if you are elderly, have a lifetime of things with memories in your home, and are living in a body that doesn't physically feel up to the task of sorting, tossing, and packing. The good news is that if everyone pitches in, it can be manageable. If everyone is not willing or able to pitch in, and there are financial resources available, there are many "senior move specialist" services available that will handle everything, from sorting through belongings to packing, to hiring the mover, to arranging the handyman to fix up the residence prior to putting it up for sale, to setting up belongings at the new home.

Options for different life stages

Independent Senior Living Facilities

When asked, many seniors will say that they would prefer to stay in their own home with assistance, as needed. Moving to a smaller home, such as an apartment or a townhome or condo with the financial resources for a caregiver, may be a great option. Keep in mind that 24-hour a day caregivers are very expensive; and even at a very meager rate of $12 an hour, you are still looking at spending over $5000 to $7000 a month for 24-hour a day care, plus "nanny taxes" that you will have to pay. Don't forget to add in the usual living expenses that we all have. There are other options for independent senior living, and those would be found in senior retirement communities. Independent senior living might be appropriate for someone with very early Alzheimer's disease or dementia who can still live independently, but can't manage an entire house. In these communities, seniors live in apartments of varying square footage with a tiny kitchen (because it isn't used much), and residents go to a restaurant-style community dining room for most of their meals. There are buses for transportation around town, and plenty of time for activities and socialization, which is excellent for someone with cognitive decline.

Senior living communities may be on a rental by the month basis, or they may be part of a "continuing care community" where there is a buy-in fee. The advantage of the rental communities are that loved ones can move from one community to another without financial penalty. For example, when an adult child gets a job transfer from Michigan to Arizona, her elderly dad can move from his senior rental community near his daughter in Michigan to one close to where his daughter is moving to in Arizona, keeping the two of them close together at all times. Independent senior communities will often also offer assisted living if that should become necessary. How would you know if it's time to move for a loved one to move to assisted living? Even in senior independent living situation, staff will still unobtrusively monitor the condition of the resident's apartment; whether they're grooming themselves; acting appropriately; how much they're eating; and any atypical behaviors are reported and monitored in weekly staff meetings. So even in "independent" living communities, there is oversight by staff for the purposes of safety.

Senior continuing care retirement communities, better known as CCRCs. In order to move into a CCRC, there is a buy-in fee, which can vary in price (depending on the place) from roughly 100,000 to over a million dollars. In addition to the buy-in fee, you will often also pay a monthly "fee" to live there. The advantage of a continuing care community is that, even if you run out of money, they will continue to care for you and allow you to live there for the rest of your life. Continuing care communities will typically offer a full spectrum of living situations: *independent senior living, assisted living, memory care, and a skilled nursing facility.* One caveat is that the Continuing Care Retirement Community will decide where you belong in the community. Even if you don't feel ready for the skilled nursing facility; that is where you'll be living if the administration there decides that's where you belong. The savvy shopper at a CCRC will probably wonder, what happens if I die a month after I move in? Am I out the huge buy-in that I paid last month? The answer can vary. Some CCRCs offer a "money back" buy-in fee (typically higher than the 'no money back' fee because you then have the option of moving out or getting buy-in money back when you die). Be sure and do your homework before signing on the bottom line for a CCRC. Have an attorney look over the contract carefully. They are a big investment, but with potential for a lot of long-term security with the assurance of lifetime care.

Assisted-Living Facilities

Assisted-living is an intermediate between independent living and living at a skilled nursing facility. They are typically staffed 24-hours a day, and residents can choose what level of assistance they'd like. Some examples would be assistance with dressing, bathing, meals, or medication reminders. The federal government does not regulate assisted-living facilities. Costs for assisted-living will vary by the facility, and not all of them are set up specifically for patients with memory loss. You need to ask the right questions when checking out these facilities. (Alzheimer's Association, 2016)

Memory Care Facilities

It seems that on nearly every corner, a memory care facility, sometimes also referred to as a special care unit, is being built. It is quite clear that there is a growing need for these facilities; many people are living longer and with increasing age, there are increasing numbers of persons with Alzheimer's disease. Statistically, 38 percent of persons, 85-years old have Alzheimer's disease and 1 in 9 elderly persons has Alzheimer's disease. (Alzheimer's Association) Many nursing homes also offer memory care in a special care unit where patients with memory loss are grouped together. Staff in special care units should be specifically trained in memory care, offer activities for persons with memory challenges, and be skilled in handling behavioral issues. (Alzheimer's Association, 2016) Many states require special care units to disclose what type of specialized care they offer; please ask for their Special Care Unit Disclosure form when you visit for more information.

Skilled Nursing Facilities

If your or your loved one does require skilled nursing care that is beyond the scope of assisted living, it can be daunting to even think about where to start looking. Did you know that Medicare doesn't pay for long-term care in a skilled nursing facility? They will only pay for 100- days after a hospitalization; afterwards, the cost falls on the patient. If you don't have money for the SNF, you will need to apply for Medicaid, and then find a good nursing home that accepts Medicaid. Some good news is that the Medicare.gov website has some helpful resources to help you select a skilled nursing facility (better known as a SNF, pronounced "sniff" by health professionals). First, at the Medicare.gov website, check out the SNF checklist (www.medicare.gov/files/skilled-nursing-facility-checklist.pdf).

The SNF Checklist is a document composed of a series of 'yes' and 'no' questions to be answered as you visit each skilled nursing facility (SNF). You will need to print a separate checklist for each SNF you're planning to visit. The questions are designed to evaluate the quality of the nursing home, and to help you decide if this facility might be a good fit for you personally. Many of the questions on the checklist are ones you may not think to ask on your own; be sure you check it out. If you visit a facility that seems to fit your needs, it's a good idea to place your name on the waiting list even if you're not sure you want to move your loved one there. Many of the good facilities have long waiting lists. You'll also want to ask what happens if your loved one runs out of money; do they accept Medicaid? You'll also want to check out "Nursing Home Compare" at the Medicare.gov website (www.medicare.gov/nhcompare/). Use the nursing home compare information, and combine that with the information gathered on your visits and recorded on your SNF Checklist to help you find a SNF that is of good quality and a good fit for your loved one.

It is common for families to struggle with the decision of whether it is the right thing to do to place their loved one in a residential facility. We've adapted these questions from the Alzheimer's Association to get you thinking. (Alzheimer's Association, 2016)

Tips to Equip: When to consider alternate living arrangements

- Is my loved one becoming unsafe in their current home?

- Is the health of the person or my health as a caregiver at risk?

- Are the person's care needs beyond my physical abilities?

- Am I becoming a stressed, irritable and impatient caregiver?

- Am I neglecting work responsibilities, my family and myself?

- Would the structure and social interaction at a care facility benefit the person with the health issues?

It is normal to feel a range of emotions when placing your loved one in any type of facility after living in their own home. Most families find it best to make the decision and swiftly move forward. The safety of our loved one is at stake, and the risks are just too great not to act. This is something we enjoy helping families navigate more easily, as it is frightening and frustrating for everyone. Often, aging parents may listen to professionals in ways they will not listen to their own families. It's all in how the message is presented, and it must be presented with compassion and fairness to all in a loving, respectful manner.

Section V

Complementary and Alternative Medicine Therapy (CAM)

This section explores alternative therapies, as a method of treating many ailments. While Western medicine remains prevalent in modern health care, there are too many cases where holistic doctors have helped patients manage pain and recover from illness to discount this method of health care.

Danny McLane is a Doctor of Chiropractic Medicine and practices in northern Illinois, Libertyville. Many people do not even realize how much more chiropractors do than make spinal adjustments to help manage pain. I think their real value is in their vast knowledge of integrative health. When I say integrative, I mean nontraditional methods to heal the human body: things like chiropractic adjustments, acupuncture, Reiki, massage therapy, ultrasonic treatments, and most importantly, nutrition. Nutrition is God's gift to the human body. People who eat well and exercise have tapped into the best possible way to support your body's innate ability to heal itself. Traditional methods may fail to bring actual healing, and many people come to Danny "when all else fails."

Why not start the healing process with the safest, lowest risk and most effective way to bring about natural healing first? I have seen, firsthand, what nontraditional methods can do. Osteopathic physicians and doctors of chiropractic medicine have much more training in nutrition and spinal pathology than medical doctors. They help people avoid dangerous cocktails of high-risk medicines that often do more harm than good when they are used carelessly.

Danny is one of the smartest, most enthusiastic chiropractors I know and I would never hesitate to refer my clients to him for treatment or nutritional support and counseling. He works well with traditional modalities as well and I am proud to give him this space to share his magic on paper.

Chapter 9

Exploring Alternative Therapies

Options for Alternative Therapies

Many major medical centers around the country are now combining conventional Western medicine with alternative or complementary treatments such as naturopathic supplements; acupuncture; massage; biofeedback; yoga; meditation; stress reduction; and organic nutritional support. The holistic model of care aims to treat the whole person instead of just the disease. Traditional Western medicine proponents refer to this approach as "complementary" to emphasize that such treatments are used *with* mainstream medicine, not as replacements or alternatives.

The American Hospital Association says that the number of hospitals that offer complementary therapies has more than tripled in the last decade, and more hospitals are planning to add complementary therapies and/or departments in the near future. (AHA.org) Several studies show that these therapies can greatly reduce unpleasant symptoms associated with chemotherapy, for some patients. They reduce pain, nausea, anxiety, and even promote healing in post-surgical patients.

Cancer Treatment Centers of America is one well-known proponent of integrative medicine. Their surgeons and oncologists routinely work side-by-side with staff naturopaths and pharmacists to make certain that patients receive a full array of complementary modalities. Acupuncture, massage, chiropractic care, Reiki therapy and even laughter therapy are offered at CTCA by the mind-body medicine department. A large pastoral care team makes certain that all patients have support to pray and meditate as they heal, and superior patient satisfaction is cited year after year. (Cancercenter.com)

Northwestern Memorial Hospital is another well-known major medical center that is known for its cutting-edge integrative medicine department, as well as Duke University and hundreds of other centers around the country that recognize the huge impact that integrative medicine has in our society. The Oster Center for Integrative Medicine in San Francisco at the University of California has joined with Harvard, Columbia, and dozens of other academic medical centers to form the Consortium of Academic Health Centers for Integrative Medicine.

The field of holistic, integrative medicine is no longer considered fringe or affiliated with hippie vegans. It is here to stay!

Alternative Medicine – A Different Perspective

By Danny McLane

Integrative medicine, holistic medicine, natural medicine...so many ways to describe taking care of the body in a way that is complementary to how the body heals itself, in most cases, without any need for Western medicine.

When Teri asked me to write a chapter related to Integrative Medicine, I thought, "Sure, but it will be like a drop of water in the ocean." Since we have just a chapter to get into a very broad and deep topic, let's jump on in.

If it ain't broke...

I do not oppose the current standard of Western Medical Care even though I may sound contrary to that in the next few statements. What I am contrary to is, Dogma–accepting the current model just because it's been accepted or because we've become accustomed to it. The use of Over-The-Counter (OTC) medications is incredibly prevalent. One recent report by Information Resources Inc. (IRI) stated that in 2015 there were 2.9 billion trips to retail outlets to buy OTC meds. These medications offer people the ability to reduce their pain and their symptoms. Some of these medications even allow people to *recover* from the minor issues that caused them to turn to OTCs in the first place. In many houses all over the country, if you look for a medicine cabinet, you're sure to find one–it's a common standard.

Then there's prescription medication, which has to be prescribed by a doctor. Those are fairly common as well, especially in the instance of the need for drugs that address common conditions. These drugs can range from statins for cholesterol to something more extreme, such as chemotherapy drugs for cancer. We often see the concept in practice of, "a pill for any ill," but has this concept gotten out of hand? I don't think so. I know many well-intentioned doctors who have their heart and head in the right place, which is squarely in line with the best interest of their patients. It's my opinion that we're missing a step in the process. We'll cover more on that as we go.

How bad can it be?

Pretty bad, it turns out. According to the Centers for Disease Control, poisoning, by drugs, is the number one cause of injury-related death in the United States. That includes, taking (or giving) too much of a substance that was not intended to cause harm.

Let that sink in.

The reality is, drugs kill more people every year than you can imagine. An estimated 280,000 people die from accidental drug-related deaths every year. This is not meant to shock you, but to help shift your perspective. Paracelsus, the father of toxicology is most memorably noted for saying, "The dose makes the poison."

In our modern culture we simply take too many drugs. Let me rephrase that, we rely on drugs to solve problems that they should not be relied upon for. How do we know? Even though America is less than the five percent of the world's total population, we consume 80 percent of opioid painkillers produced in the world. Couple that fact with the fact that, for health, we rank worst of all developed countries. Dead last. Not only did our model produce the worst outcomes, it was also the most expensive.

What about cancer? I know, it's a tough topic to discuss. My aunt died from cancer-related complications, even after being treated with chemo, twice. It makes me sad and angry, yet courageous and eager to find better solutions. But should it upset me? Should I be angry if chemo couldn't beat her cancer? Truthfully, the answer is no–not if I read the research. The part where it says that it only works 2.1 percent of the time, but it fails 97.9 percent of the time to provide a cure that lasts more than five years. Alas, here I am. I am upset that I don't get to see my aunt, or introduce her to my children, or make new memories of the good times with her. So let's soldier on and see where this leads us.

The big 'C,' that's too big of a hill to climb. What about something easier, less lethal, such as pain? There is a whole classification of drugs that are called Non-Steroidal Anti-Inflammatories (NSAIDS). They make up most of what people buy and use for common aches and pains of everyday life. Things like lower back pain, headaches, neck pain and so on. Something so mundane should be easily handled by what we've been using, right? The answer is a double-edged sword.

In a study done with over 114,000 teachers in California, the evidence shows that there was an increased risk of breast cancer from daily use of ibuprofen or aspirin over five years. For Ibuprofen the risk increased by 50 percent, and for aspirin, the risk increased by 80 percent. The pills reduce pain, but increase the risk of breast cancer.

This classification of drugs carries with it a significant risk of heart-related death as well. What's worse is the increased risks were not related to lengthy periods of time for the use of the drug either. There have been studies that reported that people taking the drugs for at least six months were dying at twice the rate of others who were not taking them. The risk was the worst with people who used Ibuprofen. They die at three times the rate of non-NSAID users. That's a 200 to 300 percent increased risk of death from heart attack, stroke, or other heart-related problem.

I realize that this is all a little shocking, but in reality, it's only a symptom of a sick system. In fairness, they are doing the best they can with what they have. They, the people, are saving lives. But why, then, are people so sick, so lost, so disappointed?

Most disease is a natural reaction to an unnatural environment

I know I hit the facts pretty hard up front, but bear with me. I have a few stories to share to illustrate my point, and I think that you'll enjoy them.

Jessie was a woman in her early forties. She had a robust fervor for life. She took college classes, not because she wanted to get a degree, but to challenge her mind. She worked out six days a week to keep her body fit and healthy. She was a health food enthusiast, who kept her house and her diet clean. She had a loving husband and daughter. She was the model of health... until she wasn't healthy anymore. Her cancer set in suddenly and without warning. Jessie's health degraded very quickly. She sought out the very best in medical care, drew her family close and did everything she could to survive.

Ben, on the other hand, was a man in his late fifties. He was a little overweight, but not unhealthy. He had a busy life as a computer programmer. He never paid much attention to what he ate or to exercise. One aspect that he did get right was time off. He often took vacations with his wife and children. His health predicament started when his right hand stopped working. In fact, everything from his shoulder to his first row of knuckles on his right hand stopped functioning altogether. Nothing seemingly caused it. When Ben came to my office, he'd already been "everywhere." He told me that he tried everything. "Everything" cost him eight months and $10,000. He still didn't know what caused it, or how to fix it. His wife made sure that he had the best medical attention to help him solve his problem. Everything from nerve testing, CT scans and MRIs. The doctors found nothing. By all accounts he should have been able to move his arm freely, yet he couldn't. He was losing hope. He wasn't nearly as hopeless as another man I treated.

When Jeff came into my office he wasn't looking for a treatment for himself. He had already resigned himself to a life of pain. He was there accompanying his daughter, who hurt her back practicing golf. She had aspirations of becoming a professional golfer. Her parents wanted the absolute best for her, and were coming to see me as a last resort. They didn't like the options that her orthopedist gave her. The physical therapy they had already tried didn't help. During the interview, we started down a line of conversation that eventually led to us talking about Jeff and his back. He was training his daughter because he had been very good at golf, before his back went out. As you can imagine, Jeff had a loss of hope for his condition. He was there for his daughter; he never really asked if I could help him. He just assumed that it was too late for him to have a normal life. He was plagued by extreme fatigue. He had enough energy to get up brush his teeth, get dressed and go downstairs; but before he could prepare breakfast for himself, he had to stop between the bedroom and the kitchen for a nap to get his energy back. Imagine the mental pain and loss of hope this man had, which brings to my next topic that we need to cover, for frame of reference.

The psychology of illness

One of the greatest quotes on optimism came from a politician who had just recently taken office as the mayor of Orange County California. She said, "Just because we've destroyed 90 percent of everything, doesn't mean we can't do amazing things with the remaining 10 percent." What she was talking about was maintaining optimism in the face of a very broken down system. There was an obvious spin to her comment. She was trying to emphasize the little positive that was left.

Buckminster Fuller, the father of modern nanotechnology, has been quoted as saying, "You never change things by fighting the existing reality. To change something, build a new model that makes the existing model obsolete."

The psychology of illness prevents us from finding a proper solution. It also encourages us to accept the standard of living that we see all around us. The number of times that I hear somebody attributing a breakdown in his or her body to normal aging is staggering. Many studies on conformity in a social setting show us just this. People tend to think that what is common is normal. It tells me that, as a population, we have a perception problem.

It's not supposed to be this way

What if we do nothing? This is a normal option that I offer to my patients all the time. In fact, doing nothing is the right option for treating certain conditions. My professor of radiology used to call certain x-ray findings "leave me alone" lesions. Referring to the best method of care was to ignore it. But is that the best option in this case? I say no.

Ask Questions

My massage therapy instructor always used to harp on us. Every class. He'd say "If the only tool you have is a hammer, every problem looks like a nail, and you won't know what to do with a screw! Get more tools in your tool box." Seriously, every class we heard this. It made me constantly ask questions, some of which I didn't even need an answer for at the time. It served me later on in my career and in my personal life. I found courage to ask questions as well as seek more options.

Where to start

The first question most people want to ask is, "what are my alternatives?" I know it took a while to get to the good stuff. Everyone wants to jump right in to what Integrative Medicine has to offer, without knowing why it's so important. Please forgive me if you had already come to that conclusion without my preamble. In Chinese medicine, they ask the question, "Can you eat bitter? Can you endure the bitter, so you'll recognize the sweetness?" If you were to ask about the alternatives first, you would have missed another step.

Teri Dreher

Master the basics first

So many disciplines of medicine skip ahead to the fancy, exotic stuff, and overlook the basics. To miss the small stuff, is to miss the big stuff. This is *my* perspective, because, as Doctor of Chiropractic, I have more training in normal physiology than any other discipline of medicine, which differs from medical doctors in that they specialize in prescribing medication.

We spend the majority of our time learning how the body is supposed to work. We master the basics. We do this so that we can notice when it's not functioning properly. Once we find it, we can define it and start our work to solve these issues. This approach is vitally important to medicine. A problem well-defined; is a problem half-solved. What you can do is to look to the common things of everyday life first, and make sure that they are in order.

The Big Idea

The body is a self-healing, self-regulating organism. It needs no help, just no interference. It makes no mistakes, but has limitations, which is the most important frame of reference you can have when approaching health. B.J. Palmer, who developed chiropractic, called it the 'Big Idea.' He was known to say, "Get the big idea, and everything else will follow."

The body is formed at conception, when a sperm and an egg connect, with the spark of life. These two half-cells become one whole cell, and start to divide. We are multitrillion cellular organisms with highly specialized cells. The human does that all without intervention from an outside influence. Our bodies grow and heal all by themselves.

Our body will do what it does, so long as there is no interference. This interference comes in the form of negative thoughts, traumas, toxins and extreme temperature. These are the only four categories of stress. We all know thoughts and feelings can help heal, or hurt. Physical traumas can leave a lifelong burden on our body, unless properly cared for. These injuries can be acute, such as a fall or crash or chronic, as in poor posture or repeated misuse of a joint. Injuries can also be a side-effect of a life-saving procedure. Surgical scars impact the tissue for years afterwards. Toxins, such as lead, or cigarette smoke are obvious; or insidious as with recycled water, or plastics; temperature is usually pretty obvious. Without the destructive force of interference, the body heals naturally.

It makes no mistakes, but has limitations

The innate intelligence of the body knows exactly how to grow a kidney, or repair a damaged eyeball, or digest your food, yet sometimes this doesn't happen. The question is why. If you want to build a brick house, you need bricks. You also need a bricklayer. Otherwise you either have a pile of bricks, or a guy standing around without supplies. In order to build a healthy body, it requires good nutrition/ chemical building blocks (structure) and properly working physiology (function).

If the limitation on health and growth is chemical (structure) in nature, as in poor nutrition, health will suffer. This is beautifully showcased in the documentary, *"Fat, Sick and Nearly Dead, by Joe Cross (April 1, 2011)."* The subject of the documentary, Joe, was very successful in life, but he had poor health. His body was struggling for health because he lacked the raw materials for basic cell function and repair. He recovered his health by drinking juiced vegetables and fruit. As he nourished his body, the limitations on his health resolved and he healed.

If the limitation on health and growth is physiologic (function) in nature; as seen when a person has a bone out of place, putting pressure on a spinal nerve, causing it to dysfunction, health will also suffer. Standard medical science shows that nerve interference can affect every function in the body. Proper nerve function is how the brain keeps the body functioning. It's almost scary to realize that pressure equal to the weight of a dime, 2.28g, can cause a nerve to dysfunction by 60 percent.

The intent of this work is not to be an exhaustive walk through all of Integrative Medicine, but a glimpse as to what else is available to you and your loved ones seeking health. Now that we have the Big Idea, let's build on it.

What are the basics?

When we look at the body as healing and self-regulating, food comes to mind as an obvious starting point right? Actually, the most important starting point is the major system of control in the body, which is the nervous system. It controls and coordinates every function in the body. Simply stated, everyone needs to get checked and corrected by a chiropractor because we are specialized in restoring proper function to the nervous system.

The job of the nervous system is to adapt our bodies to the stresses we encounter in everyday life. Without it, we die. Without the nervous system functioning at optimal levels, we simply can't function at our best. That means every system within the body suffers–the heart, lungs, immune and digestive systems, muscles bones, joints, nerves, EVERY, single cell. To ensure you are working with all the odds in your favor, I recommend enlisting the help of a chiropractor.

Don't underestimate the importance of good nutrition

The simplest, most accurate comment about food that I have heard is the following statement, "Eat food, mostly plants, not too much." This means you need food–Real food, not food-products. The Standard American Diet (SAD) is comprised of 63 percent empty calories with no nutritional benefit. It is no wonder people are sick with any manner of lifestyle disease.   There is no such thing as health food or junk food. There is food, and then there is junk. Just because you *can* eat it, doesn't mean you *should*. All real food is health food. If it's not food, it's junk. The body is resilient, so people can get away with eating junk, for a long time. The body will compensate as much as it can, for as long as it can. Once it can't, it won't. Unfortunately, by the time symptoms of poor health show up, all the back up plans have been exhausted and the body has entered into a state of "biological debt." The answer lies in eating well. This is the second most important thing you can do for your health.

You're not sick, you're thirsty

This is not just the catch phrase of a fantastic book. These are words to live by. Water is the universal solvent. It dissolves and carries the majority of chemistry we need to perform most biological functions in the body. You need water for that. The only way the food we eat gets to where it's going in our body is by a river of blood. You need water for that. When we eat a full meal, our body uses the fluid from our blood, about 75 percent of the total volume, for digestion. Most of that water is added in the form of saliva and digestive juices. Then it's reabsorbed in the colon. You need water for that.

A general guideline for a healthy individual is 2 to 2.5 liters of water per day, plus enough to offset any diuretics, such as coffee, tea and alcohol. Dehydration can be defined as a one percent or greater loss of body mass due to fluid loss.

A body in motion

Movement is an important key to life. Blood flows out to the body from the heart in order to sustain life. This is an active pump. The return of blood from the body to the heart is passive. The same is true for the lymphatic fluid. Your lymphatic system acts as a sewer system in the body, draining off the waste. This is also true of the fluid that nourishes our joints, all of them. The same goes for our fluid that nourishes the brain and spinal system. All of these systems are only effective at cleaning and feeding the body when the body moves. The bowels have some natural motion, but are aided greatly when the body, as a whole, moves. The heart is one muscular pump. All the other muscles play the role of muscular pump for all the other fluids

So then, it makes perfect sense to assume that anything that keeps you moving is good for your health. We see that evidenced by scientific studies. They show that exercise is beneficial for sleep, memory, strength, power, balance, functionality, reduced pain, lower blood pressure, reduced psychiatric symptoms, and really this list could just keep going. These are but a small fraction of how exercise helps the body and mind stay healthy. If ever there was a doubt, it should be clear by now that exercise is a key to health.

Time waits for no one

In the book, *"Younger Next Year,"* Chris Crowley and Henry S. Lodge M.D. discuss how living with health as a mindset can reverse the biological effects of aging. This is true. In my clinic, I see youthful elderly and aged youth. I also witness the recovery of function that was lost to "normal aging" regularly. As we covered before, interference affects us all and diminishes our total capacity. So be aware that many signs or complaints that gather as one ages, are simply due to lack of proper maintenance. The body will heal if it is given what it needs.

Time is a catalyst; it allows you to do more of what you are doing. If the impact of your choices is negative, your health becomes more negative. When you start choosing more healthful options, your health recovers. This is where many people get stuck. It happens to everyone, "but I've been doing it for years," or "it's never made a difference before" are phrases commonly used when someone is in denial of a bad habit that is taking away their health.

Imagine, if you will, that you are in an airplane, cruising at 30,000 feet. If you lose 1000 feet, not much of anything happens. However, if you repeat that drop in altitude every 10 minutes, the effects will be more tangible. If the windows on the plane were covered, you wouldn't realize there was an issue until the landing gear of the plane started hitting the tops of the tallest trees. In health, this is when symptoms start. Not at the beginning, when you first lose altitude, but near the end, just before a crash. Be proactive. Start now. Get time on your side.

A problem well-defined is a problem half-solved

There is no sense being at the top of the wrong ladder. In health care, there are options. Many times there is a rift between what you will be told in a hospital setting and the Complementary and Alternative Medicine (CAM) setting. This rift is simply a lack of understanding. The science is all there. I will lay out for you a few examples of literally thousands, where the CAM treatments are the BEST option. Not just in terms of safety, but *real* results. Sometimes you can be your own guru, and find these options for yourself. Many times you need an expert to navigate the complexities of options availed to you. Teri and I agree that the best way to help people is to empower and equip them. It's one of the many reasons I respect her approach. She does a wonderful job helping people understand not only what can be done; but what *else* can be done. This is one of the reasons I offer a free daily health update to all my clients. A well-informed patient is one who can help themselves. It puts power in the hands of people who want to be healthy.

Any help will help

This is a danger in health care. There is a phenomenon that happens in people, not just doctors, nurses and health care workers. It's called search satisfaction. It is the tendency of a person to stop searching once they find a solution. This is a great help if you're looking for a lost set of keys, but it can be outright disastrous in health care. Why? Any help will help, but the right help, in the right way, will help the most. A human is not a standardized unit.

According to the book, *Grays Anatomy,* the largest segment of the population that matches each other anatomically is 22 percent. Every other group represented is 18 percent or less. This just further accentuates the complexity of the human condition.

There exists a significant amount of variability in people, and the way they function. So how does this apply? In, *The 7 Habits of Highly Effective People,* the author, Stephen Covey, uses the phrase "nothing fails like success." His implication is that success doesn't generalize out of context. What works for one person may not work for another. Oftentimes, it will not work for the *same* person at a different time.

To correlate that perspective to search satisfaction, the picture that starts to form is a grim one. We go back to the saying, "If the only tool you have is a hammer, every problem looks like a nail." This is one of the biggest problems in health care that Integrative Medicine addresses. When people get hurt, they want a solution. They trust their doctors to lead them to the best option. And doctors do, don't they? In a huge study of workers with back pain, that answer became very clear. Of people who went to a surgeon, 42.7 percent had back surgery. Of people who went to a Doctor of Chiropractic, 1.5 percent had surgery.

This isn't to imply that surgeons are bad doctors, not at all. They are great doctors. They are great at what they do, but they are not always great at what they don't do. There's an old adage in the health care field that says, "What you're not up on, you're down on." Basically, you endorse and support what you know.

That's great if you are looking to buy a new pair of shoes, or giving recommendations for a good restaurant in town. But this is major. Every doctor takes an oath that begins, "First, do no harm." No one is going to argue that a life-saving surgery comes with acceptable risks, but what about a less invasive, safer way to solve the same problem? Remember, drugs are not without danger either. In 2010, 38,329 people died from pharmaceutical drugs or prescription opioid drugs. As compared to chiropractic, that, during the course of about 100 clinical trials, has not had a single patient experience or a major adverse side effect. This is only to emphasize that other options are available and should be used first. You can always get multiple opinions before making your choice.

Confidence in an inadequate solution prevents participation in an adequate solution.

Options limit choices and choices limit outcomes. Now that we have come this far into our time together, let's look back and see the finality of the three stories we started earlier on in the chapter. We have a clearer perspective as to why integrative health care is essential.

Jeff, the gentleman who had back pain but was more concerned about his daughter. Let's start with him. The reason he had lost hope for his back pain was because he was told he couldn't be helped. He had a panel of nine specialists at a prestigious hospital system review his case. These specialists did everything they knew to do, to help him. They sent him to a bigger, even more prestigious hospital for further testing and evaluation. They told him the same message. They gave him a diagnosis of Transverse Myelitis. TM is usually only found at one nerve level, and only on one side of the body. Jeff had it at every level, on both sides.

I agreed with the "-itis part" of his diagnosis. He was certainly inflamed. So I dug in deeper. I did something radical and I asked him what he ate. None of his other doctors talked to Jeff about food. He told me that because of his condition he ate whatever his wife made for dinner and some easy things throughout the day. He used the term junk food. I corrected him. "Jeff, it's just junk, there's no food in that," I said. He agreed to make a significant change in his diet, mostly because he was desperate and it was a change that both he and his daughter needed, but I kept digging.

I asked him what hobbies he was involved in, what sports he played and if he had a history of injury. It was messy. He had an extensive history with a lot of suspect behaviors. All that could have caused his issues. I asked him what he did for a living before he was disabled. He shared that he had been working in an office a few years. He'd had to get an office job after his lower back started to bother him while he was finishing a concrete flooring project. I had a moment when it hit me. I asked what kind of finishing he was doing. "Epoxy, mostly" was his reply.

I had a flashback to my Organic Chemistry 2 class. Epoxides are an extremely volatile and reactive species of compound. They are used in industry to make a reaction happen to make a combination of liquids react into a solid. He'd been breathing these compounds into his lungs. The nerves that go to the lungs are between the ribs, on both sides, at every level of the thoracic spine. That was it. He had epoxide poisoning. That explained why the adjusting helped, and the massage helped and the pool therapy helped. But none of them solved his issue. He needed a nutritional intervention. Not drugs, not body work. I recommended he watch the documentary *Fat Sick and Nearly*

Dead, and start on vegetable juice right away. He did. In less than three months, he was out golfing again. So he stopped juicing. His pain came back, although, this time not as harsh, so he began again. The pain stopped again. He asked me, "Doc, how long do I have to juice?" I replied, "Does it matter; you're living your life now, right?"

What about Ben? The programmer whose right arm shut off. Who really knows what happened? I set aside about an hour to work with him the first visit because I had no idea how it would go. After he ran down his list of interventions that he tried, and my list of common issues, which happen commonly, all was but exhausted. So I decided to use Applied Kinesiology (AK) to map out what was functioning and what was not. Now, AK looks odd, because it's not a very well known technique. Rather than attempting to explain all the intricacies, I just went about my work. It's a system that uses reflex points to help focus the brain on nerve pathways so they function better. Sure enough, after 45 minutes of Ben telling me I was rubbing the wrong spot, that his leg had nothing to do with his shoulder, he proclaimed his need to visit my restroom. When he stood up, he pushed himself up with both hands, and walked to the restroom. Didn't even notice. When he came out, he reached back and swung the door closed, with his right hand. Then looked at me and asked, "Ok, what's next?" Didn't even notice. So I asked, "Hey Ben, what hand did you zip up with?" This request made him focus on his right arm. He raised his hand up, in front of his face and wiggled his fingers around. His face paled; I thought he was going to pass out. He looked at me and asked, "What did you do?" This was in my first few years of practice when I was a bit more spry. I replied,

"You asked me to fix your arm, I fixed your arm...TADA IT'S MAGIC!"

Ben is catholic. Magic of this kind was voodoo, and not acceptable. After that, I tried to explain to him that it was actually advanced neuroscience. But between the disbelief that a guy, with no technology, could solve a problem that the best hospital care didn't, coupled with my foot-in-mouth comment about magic, he wasn't really receptive to any kind of scientific explanation. Not even if it was about how stimulatory and inhibitory neural networks regulated afferent fibers that... nope. I lost him. He went home to his wife, who had extensive training in rehab as an Occupational Therapist, and told her I was a witch doctor.

But what of Jessi? She died. The second round of chemo was too much for her to handle. The first round helped her fight off cancer but left her immune system devastated. It also radicalized her cancer. The chemo killed off all the daughter cells, but made the mother cells more effective at resisting any kind of therapy. She was my aunt. I love her and I still miss her.

When you know better, you do better
When most of my clients ask me for an alternative to pain meds they expect that I will give them a recommendation for a watered down natural option. They expect that my efforts will only result in a shadow of what the "heavy duty" pharmaceuticals can deliver. In fact, one of my 'go-to' options is curcumin. It's an herbal extract from turmeric. There are 9,258 scientific studies in Pubmed.gov database at the time of this writing to show its efficacy. It is better at lowering high cholesterol than Atorvastatin; better than corticosteroids for decreasing inflammation; better than

Prozac and Imipramine for depressive behavior; better as a blood thinner than Aspirin; better as an anti-inflammatory than aspirin, ibuprofen, sulindac, phenylbutazone, naproxen, indomethacin, diclofenac, dexamethasone, celecoxib, and tamoxifen; 500-100,000 times better than Metformin at treating type 2 diabetes; better than Oxaliplatin as an anti-proliferative cancer drug. The best known compound for chemotherapy-resistant and radiation-resistant cancers, and that's the short list. That's also just one example of hundreds. Better options are out there.

A great big world
The world of physiology changes every six months. It is not a static topic like math. It is constantly changing in major ways. It changes so rapidly that, over time, it's easy to be stuck with yesterday's news, holding in high esteem many conventional wisdoms that have been proven dead wrong. Did you hear about how the FDA reversed its recommendation for a daily aspirin? They cited that the actual harm outweighed the potential benefits. I read between 10-25 articles per day to stay current. I also offer a daily health update to all of my clients for free, so they can stay current as well. In preparing to write this chapter, I pulled from my collection of research articles about 600 of the most interesting, relevant new bits of news from the world of science and health care. Obviously, I can't share even a fraction of them in this small space. So you see my friends, I have not presented to you a drop of water in the ocean, but instead, the ocean in a drop of water. Explore. Read. Ask questions.

Tips to Equip: Considering Alternative Medicine

- More respected medical facilities have complementary medicine specialties to work with Western medicine than ever before; don't be afraid to have the "alternative medicine" discussion with your physician

- Never underestimate the importance of good nutrition

- Don't be a slave to Dogma

- Most disease is a natural reaction to an unnatural environment

- Some illnesses can be improved by beginning with a change in your perception

- Your body has the innate ability to self-regulate and self-heal without interference, but it does have limitations

- Water is a universal solvent; sometimes that's all the body needs

- Movement is an important key to life

✑ Section VI ✑

Documents and Insurance: What You Need To Know

I left this section as the last one in the book on purpose. Throughout the previous sections, I've touched on the importance of putting legal documents in place as well as shared some examples of the ill-effects of not keeping your documents up to date; this was especially true in Caroline's case. I will delve a little deeper into this subject in the *Legal Documents* section. As hard as it is to tackle, this is a subject that must be addressed as more and more people are suffering medical catastrophes to the point where they become incompetent to continue making decisions for their life and welfare. Whether that is due to mental incapacity, medical malaise or even death, the importance of having legal documents in place to carry out your wishes has never been more important. I will discuss how simple and stress-free it can be with the right team in place.

This section also gives more insight into the Affordable Care Act of 2010 or "Obama Care" as it is often referred. As you read further, you will become aware of more intricacies of legal documents and the different options in modern health care as it relates to insurance coverage.

I've asked Jean Lyon to contribute to this section on Medicare, as she is a trusted colleague who helps our company stay on top of the health care insurance industry, particularly as it relates to Medicare and supplements. Who new that modern health care would become so complex that even the insurance industry has subspecialties? Jean stays on top of it all and cares about her clients, as unique individuals with very different needs and challenges as the insurance landscape continues to evolve. In today's challenging health care environment, almost all insurance brokers have lost their commissions, so the public is often left to struggle on their own to keep on top of which companies are going out of states and changing their networks. It is simply too much for most seniors to navigate alone. For those who know someone with the know how to help give impartial advice on which plan will meet your needs in the coming year, you have found a real treasure. Read on to see how Jean helps untangle some of the most basic misunderstandings about Medicare, Medicaid and other supplements for seniors.

Chapter 10

Hospital 101 For The Medicare or Medicaid Patient

One of the most heartbreaking things that happens in hospitals every day is something all too common among our elderly patients. You've probably heard about it yourself: an otherwise healthy, active older patient gets admitted to the hospital for a relatively minor ailment and a cascade of events spills over and progresses rapidly. My friend's elderly aunt, at age 94, moved houses to be closer to her sister and all went well until she tripped at home and broke her hip. She went to the hospital and couldn't sleep well, so the doctor ordered a sedative that would help her sleep, but it also made her disoriented and confused. When she woke up in the middle of the night, she fell and hit her head and suffered a bleed on her brain due to the blood thinners she was taking. She was ordered to stay on bed rest and soon developed pneumonia and cardiac problems. Soon the treatment for her cardiac problems led to kidney failure. She got so sick, she stopped eating.

Once she stopped eating, more things deteriorated and she was transferred to a skilled nursing facility (SNF). The nurse admitting her could see right away that she was fragile and would probably not survive. A Do Not Resuscitate (DNR) order was entered after consulting with the family and she died shortly thereafter.

The point? Seniors do not generally do well in hospitals. Their immune systems are often weaker, they react more easily to medications, and they do not eat well. If you have a loved one in the hospital, make sure a family member is with them, to encourage them to eat and drink, offer them snacks, and take them for frequent short walks in the hallways to keep up their strength. Hospitals do not have the staff to give the same level of attention as in days past, and by the time malnutrition or muscle weakness is noticed, the first thing the discharge planner will want to do is send them to rehab or a SNF. The bottom line is that seniors, adults with disabilities, and the mentally ill are often having a harder time than most in navigating modern health care. Because healthcare providers are receiving lower reimbursement rates for Medicare/Medicaid patients, it is becoming harder for patients to find excellent doctors who are also accepting Medicare patients.

Hospitals and insurance companies, who are receiving lower reimbursement rates, are working hard to recoup the losses so they remain profitable. Since quality of care is not tied closely to future Medicare reimbursement, there are several changes in the industry that hit seniors hard. Perhaps the most common is the 30-day readmissions controversy that is part of the Affordable Care Act.

This policy was added in part to cut down on Medicare fraud and deals with the revolving-door syndrome of seniors who were frequently readmitted within the first month after an inpatient admission. Medicare feels that these readmissions are red flags and suspects that poor discharge planning took place, sending seniors back home too quickly. Too many of these red flags will affect the hospital's quality rating, and the hospital will receive lower reimbursement rates the following year. This can add up to millions of dollars annually.

The scheme that hospitals came up with to reduce their readmission stats involved admitting all questionable senior admissions under observation status. "Observation" hospitalizations are covered under Medicare Part B, which is technically not a "real" hospitalization, so the hospital is not liable to have so many red flags for repetitive inpatient readmissions. The patient usually does not even realize they are admitted under observation status. They go to a regular room and receive the same services as any full-admission patient would. There is a time limit (three midnights) for observation stays before the doctor is called upon to re-evaluate their admission status or discharge them. Currently, over 40 percent of ER patients are admitted under observation status. (Medicare. gov) Nurses and physicians are required to document patient status updates more frequently, and the cost of an observation admission is often higher than a regular admission. Medications administered during an observation stay are also not included in the hospital bill, so seniors will pay extra for them.

The real problem occurs when a senior becomes so weak during the hospital stay that inpatient rehabilitation is ordered. Medicare will not cover rehab expenses if the patient goes to rehab from an observation stay, as it is technically an outpatient stay and one cannot move from outpatient to acute inpatient rehab and have it paid for by Medicare. This has caused a huge uproar over the past three years and consumer advocacy groups have lobbied hard to protect seniors from the financial consequences of this ruling. Care managers in hospitals are supposed to keep patients informed about their admission/observation status and most of them do, but sometimes that critical piece of information gets lost in the shuffle with copies of admission paperwork and discharge forms. Patients should always verify their admission status before transferring to a rehab facility if they do not want to be surprised by getting billed by the rehab facility weeks later.

I once had a client whose mother fell into this trap. Her healthy 87-year-old mother fell at home when she tripped over her little dog. At the hospital, and with X-rays confirming that she had broken her hip, the patient had such severe postoperative pain that she did not move unless she had to and became weaker, losing her appetite, losing weight and sleeping a lot after getting frequent pain pills. One week after her surgery, she tried to go home with home health care and physical therapy ordered. Unfortunately, she fell again when getting up to go to the bathroom one night. Her daughter called 911 and the patient was readmitted under observation status. Two days later she was transferred to a local rehab facility, where she slowly made a full recovery over the next month. The client contacted us when they received a bill for over $10,000. Medicare had refused to pay because the prior hospitalization had been under observation status.

It is always easier for geriatric care managers or professional advocates to save clients money if we are called in early to oversee the patient's hospitalization. We make sure that the right questions are being asked on the front end so patients and families do not reap serious consequences on the back end when the bills come due. Although we cannot always change the admission status, at least we can ask all the right questions, crucial questions that healthcare consumers may not even be aware of, which is a critical task and perk of enlisting the help of a PPHA.

The Intricacies of Medicare
by Jean Lyon

To some, particularly those of age, Medicare can seem like a magic word. You've finally reached the long-awaited age of sixty-five. You may not be excited about turning another year older; but you are definitely excited about one thing–free health care insurance. Or is it? Unfortunately, the bad news is, Medicare is not free.

Medicare is completely different from Medicaid.
Medicare is the health insurance offered for seniors. Medicaid is public aid, a social health care program for families and individuals with low income and limited resources. It doesn't help that the place that runs Medicare also runs Medicaid–CMS, The Centers for Medicare and Medicaid Services. It's no wonder the two words are often confused.

As you happily picture opening your mailbox to see that special birthday present everyone gets at the age of sixty-five, you will find that a few steps may have been missed along the way.

The harsh reality is, unless you're already drawing Social Security at age sixty-five, a Medicare card is not going to miraculously appear in your mailbox. You must be proactive and sign up. You have three months before you turn sixty-five, the month of your birthday and three months after you turn sixty-five to sign up for Medicare. You may sign up one of three ways: 1) Go to medicare.gov, 2) Call your Social Security office, or 3) Physically visit your local Social Security office. Unfortunately, it's not like your dentist; you won't receive a friendly reminder notice in the mail that it's time to sign up, you have to do it all on your own.

Medicare Part A

Medicare only covers the premium for Medicare Part A. While it is true that, if you've worked and paid into Social Security for forty quarters (ten years), you will receive Medicare—that is only for the *premium* for Medicare Part A. Here's what no one tells you; *you have to pay for everything else.* You're still on the hook for the deductibles, co-pays, co-insurance and other premiums (more about this later).

Medicare is made up of several parts. Medicare has four parts to it; Medicare Part A (hospital), Medicare Part B (doctors), Medicare Part C (Medicare Advantage-to be discussed later) and Medicare Part D (pharmacy). While the premium for Medicare Part A is covered, you must still pay the premium for Medicare Part B and Medicare Part D. And, even with these premium payments, this still won't pay for all of your health care expenses. The premiums listed will basically cover only 80 percent of your medical care, which means you're responsible for the remaining 20 percent (that 20 percent is what the insurance types mean by 'co-pay'). In order to help offset the remainder, you will need a

Medicare supplement and even then, the average supplemental insurance will only pay 80 percent of what's left.

The hospital. Let's say you're in the hospital for ten days. Even for a relatively minor issue, that bill would very likely be— at a minimum—in the $50,000 range. If Medicare covered 80 percent, you would still be liable for $10,000. This is where the value of a Medicare Supplements comes into play. A supplement will often cover approximately 80 percent of this remaining $10,000, leaving you to pay $2,000. It's still a lot of money; but better than $10,000 and certainly better than shelling out $50,000. For people who can afford top tier supplemental insurance, the bill may be covered entirely.

The deductible. Before your Medicare Part A hospital coverage kicks in, you'll also have to pay the deductible of approximately $1,300. Bear in mind, most Medicare supplements will pay part or all of this deductible.

Please make sure you're an admitted patient; I cannot reinforce this enough. The first step is to make sure that you have been an "admitted patient" and not "under observation." This is a crucial caveat because Medicare Part A does not go into effect unless you're an "admitted patient." For example, let's say you've taken a nasty fall, you go to an emergency room and you are now "under observation." Until you are actually admitted to the hospital, Medicare Part A benefits do not begin. You will need to use your Medicare Part B coverage until you're admitted (more on Medicare Part B later).

Once you have been admitted, your first sixty days in the hospital are covered; and for the majority of people—and particularly with the pressure hospitals have of keeping patients the shortest amount of time possible—sixty days will usually be enough hospital insurance unless you have a serious chronic illness.

Rehab facility/skilled nursing. However, it doesn't mean that everything will be covered once you leave the hospital and you need to go to a rehab facility. Remember that "admitted vs. observation" issue?

Three midnights in the hospital are required for approval. If, for example, you've had a knee replacement and you need to rehab in a skilled nursing rehab facility, you have to have spent at least *three consecutive midnights* as an admitted patient at the hospital for Medicare Part A to cover your rehab stay. If you do not have three consecutive midnights, unless you have additional insurance, you will have to pay privately for your stay at the rehab facility.

Medicare only covers the first twenty days in full at the rehab facility. Medicare Part A will cover your first twenty days in full. But, after this, for days 21 to 100, Medicare Part A only provides the insured with $161 per day. But, OK, you say, *that sounds like a lot, isn't that enough?* If the daily cost for room and board at the rehab facility is $300 per day (and it's often more), this means you have to pay to the remaining $139 per day. If you were to stay the full 100 days, your share would be $11,120. However, if you do have a Medicare supplement, your share will often be reduced to $2,224—the supplement pays 80 percent of that remaining fee and you pay 20 percent of it out-of-pocket.

To qualify, you must demonstrate improvement. It can be another story if the patient discharged from the hospital is a frail elderly person or has a form of dementia. In these scenarios, it is challenging for the patient to demonstrate enough improvement to qualify for Medicare Part A. If they cannot follow instructions or they are too weak to actually rehab, the care would not be covered by Medicare.

Nursing home care. Here's a common scenario; a rushed and harried adult child comes into a retirement community. The adult child, Susie, has picked the most attractive hotel-like place she could find close to her home. And, more importantly, based on her research, this retirement place offers excellent care. She then tells the counselor the following story.

On a recent visit to her mother, Susie saw that her mother was as hale and hearty as always, but, when she opened the refrigerator, Susie was horrified to see that her mother had placed her shoes on the top shelf. To make matters worse, Susie then realizes her mother placed milk in her bedroom closet; the milk had gone sour, the stench engulfing the entire room. Alarmed, and juggling one hundred other work and home duties, Susie hurriedly did research about local retirement communities and made an appointment; this is what brought her to the meeting this morning.

After the meeting with the counselor, Susie tours the community, patting herself on the back that she has indeed made an excellent choice. In fact, because her mother is so healthy, she discovers her mother won't even have to move into the "skilled nursing" area. The person who gave her the tour informs her that her mother can move to the nice apartments called, "Assisted-Living Memory Care."

With relief, Susie pulls out her mother's Medicare card with a flourish, plops it on the table and asks to move her mother into the nice apartments today. The room grows quiet. The counselor has the unpleasant task of informing Susie that all of her mother's Assisted Living care is called, "Custodial Care," which is not covered by Medicare.

All custodial care is private pay. "Independent Living," "Assisted Living," and "Memory Care" are not covered by Medicare. In addition, and even more painful, most "Skilled Nursing Care" (what most people think of when they think of nursing home care) is not covered by Medicare.

Medicare does not cover "custodial care." Medicare only covers "acute care." This means, care when there has been an acute event; i.e. a stroke, a fall, a heart attack, etc. Unfortunately, Medicare does not pay for long-term care resulting from a chronic medical condition. When you consider that Independent Living up to Skilled Nursing care can cost between $50,000 to $100,000 respectively or more per year, this is a very sobering thought.

Medicare Part B–Office Visits

So, what is this Medicare B all about? Medicare B is insurance for doctor's visits and lab work. And, unlike Medicare Part A, for Medicare Part B, you have to pay a monthly premium. Unless you have a higher income, for most people, that would be $121.80 per month or $1,461.60 per year. In addition, there is a $161 deductible. After this, your doctor's visits, etc. would be covered 80 percent and you would be responsible for the remaining 20 percent. Again, you would need a supplement policy to cover the bulk of the remaining charges.

Medicare Part D–Prescription Drug Coverage

While most people are aware—or at least have heard of— Medicare Part B, a surprisingly large number of people are not aware of Medicare Part D, nor do they sign up for it. Is this really that big of deal? You'll see why in a minute.

Again, Medicare Part D entails an initial deductible, $360. After that, you're responsible for your monthly premium. Without getting into too much detail, Medicare A and Medicare B are called, "Original Medicare," and the federal government manages them. On the other hand, private insurance companies manage Medicare Part D. Because of this, the premiums can vary greatly; but, on average, the premium would be approximately $30 per month or $360 per year.

You're now aware of Medicare Part D but you say to yourself, "Hey, I only use one cholesterol med and it only costs about $10 a month. Why on earth should I pay an additional $30 per month?" Good question. Yes, that's what you pay now; but let's say three years down the road you (God forbid) have a major health catastrophe. You discharge from the hospital, but instead of your $10 monthly pharmacy bill, you are suddenly saddled with a whopping $1,600 monthly pharmacy bill (this sort of amount is sadly common after an acute medical event). So now, because you do have Medicare Part D—which is normally split 75 percent paid by the insurance company and your responsibility of 25 percent—your share of this pharmacy bill is $400 instead of the $1,600. Over the course of a year, if you're required to continue taking these meds each month, that would amount to well over a $14,000 savings for prescriptions alone.

If you're thinking you can just sign up for Medicare Part D when you have these mammoth pharmacy bills, Medicare is way ahead of you.

Late enrollment penalties

Like any other type of insurance, Medicare operates under the premise of everyone pooling their resources together and those pooled resources offset the care of the people drawing from the combined funds. In essence, Medicare relies on everyone signing up as soon as they are eligible. The good news is, at age sixty-five, no one can be underwritten, that means, everyone qualifies for Medicare no matter the state of their health. On the other hand, as part of this deal, Medicare is banking on many healthy individuals signing up at age sixty-five. If everyone just waited to sign up when they needed intense pharmacy or medical attention, it would unfairly place the burden on those who did sign up on time. The system would simply not work.

If you are sixty-five or older, still employed and you have credible health insurance (NOT COBRA), you do not have to sign up for Medicare yet (but the company must have twenty or more employees). You can continue using your company's insurance, or decide if you wish to receive Medicare Part A as a supplement to your current health insurance (since it won't cost you anything) and wait to enroll in Medicare Part B once you retire.

Medicare Part B, late enrollment penalties. To combat people waiting to enroll until they're sick and need the coverage, Medicare has late enrollment penalties for people who sign up late. For Medicare Part B, that penalty is 10 percent for every 12-month period you didn't sign up. In this case, if you signed up three years late, the $121.80 monthly premium rises to $121.80 x 10 percent = $12.18. $12.18 penalty x 3 = $36.54. It may seem like it's no big deal to pay $36.54, but to clarify, that's $121.80 (base fee) + $36.54 (penalty) = $158.34 **per month,** not a one-time fee. You may think, "Well, OK, that's not great, but I'll just repay that amount for the next three years." Unfortunately, that penalty is permanent. Instead of paying $121.80 per month, you're stuck with $158.34... *forever.* Not that this amount will be fixed. The base amount increases every year, so the base and penalty would increase every year. Please sign up on time.

Medicare Part D, late enrollment penalties. Now, let's look at the far more common occurrence; people signing up late for Medicare Part D. Because the monthly premiums are based on the open market, the calculation is a little more nebulous. The calculation is one percent of the average fee x the number of months. If Medicare deems the monthly average premium to be $30, one percent equals 30 cents. Now you're really thinking, "Ding me with the 30 cents, who cares?" But again, that average fee is multiplied by the number of months, i.e. 30 cents for one year = $3.60. But, you're three years late, $3.60 x 3 = $10.80. You're still thinking, "Ok, ten bucks—I'll pay it." Again, Medicare is not saying this will be a one-time penalty of $10.80. No, that fee is added to your monthly premium, $30 + $10.80 = $40.80, *every month for as long as you use Medicare.* And, just like with Medicare Part B, the base fee increases each year.

In both instances, with Medicare Part B or Medicare Part D, even if you were misinformed; didn't quite understand about the deadline; or you were rolling the dice, hoping you didn't need the insurance—and now you find you'll be dinged with a penalty... sign up anyway. Yes, it would not be pleasant to have to pay, for example 25 percent or 30 percent more for the premium, but it's a mere pittance compared to paying those future health care expenses out-of-pocket.

The Donut Hole. It would be remiss not to at least mention the infamous "Donut Hole." This used to be a much bigger problem because the size of the donut hole used to be much bigger. The donut hole refers to a coverage gap for Medicare Part D. Until your drug expenses reach $3,670 within one year; insurance pays roughly 75 percent of the bill, you pay 25 percent. After this point, you are in the donut hole. Not long ago, once you were in the coverage gap, insurance paid for nothing until your pharmacy bills reached an amount Medicare D calls "Catastrophic Coverage."

However, nowadays, insurance pays for approximately 50 percent of this "coverage gap" until the insured's expenses reach the "Catastrophic Coverage" amount of $4.850. In other words, $4,850 to $3,670 = $1,180; there is a gap of $1,180. Instead of Medicare Part D paying 75 percent of this amount, it pays approximately 50 percent of charges (and it will depend on the 'tiers' of drugs used). So, instead of paying your normal share of $295 for this amount, you're liable for $590 while in the coverage gap. Medicare is filling this hole at a rate of 10 percent per year and this gap is slated to be filled by the year 2020.

Medicare Part C. Medicare Part C replaces "Original Medicare." With "Original Medicare," you would have Medicare

Part A and Medicare Part B with a Medicare Part D policy added to it and a Medigap supplement. Medicare Part C, known as Medicare Advantage, bundles them all into one. To be clear, you still would need to pay your Medicare Part B premium, but Medicare Part C replaces Medicare Part A and Medicare Part B and includes Medicare Part D. You would not need to buy separate supplement or pharmacy insurance.

There are a couple of reasons you might want to exercise that option, but mostly it boils down to your personal preference. "Original Medicare" + Medicare Part D pharmacy coverage offers you more choices. In essence, although not all Medigap policies work this way, you're able to go to any hospital or doctor who accepts Medicare, but you pay for it. While the flexibility can be a convenient option, you pay for that Medigap policy, whether you use it or not.

A **Medicare Advantage** policy, on the other hand, operates more like an HMO or a PPO (Medicare Part C offers both of these options as well as some additional specialty plans). In the positive column, although you are restricted to a particular network, the networks are large and you often pay a low premium or no premium at all. The downside is, if you don't live in a large urban area, there can be higher initial deductibles; and, to confuse matters more, Medigap policies have to be chosen carefully because some Medigap policies do not have a Maximum Out-of-Pocket cap. All Medicare Advantage plans offer this cap. Again, it's all about your personal preference and level of comfort.

What Medicare doesn't cover. Here's something that comes as a surprise to many people transitioning into Medicare, there are several key things that Medicare doesn't cover at all. **No vision**. Medicare does not pay for optometry visits or glasses. **No dental**. Medicare does not pay for dental visits or dentures. **No hearing**. Medicare does not pay for hearing tests or, more importantly, hearing aids (which can be very pricey). Some Medicare advantage policies do cover all or part of these.

Medicare Election times

There are basically four time periods when you can make your Medicare choices:

- **Initial Enrollment Period**
  - ◊ -3 months before you turn 65
  - ◊ -The month of your birthday
  - ◊ -3 months after you turn 65
  - ◊ -7 months total

The great news about this *Initial Enrollment Period*, as detailed before, you cannot be disqualified for pre-existing conditions.

What if you miss these deadlines?

- **General Enrollment Period**
  - ◊ January 1 to March 31
  - ◊ Coverage begins July 1st

You use this time to sign up for Medicare Part A and Part B, but don't forget about Part D.

If you enroll late for Part D, you'll have to wait for Special Enrollment, April 1 to June 30 or for Open Enrollment.

- **Open Enrollment Period** (also called **Annual Enrollment Period**)
    ◊ Oct. 15th to Dec. 7th
    ◊ "Preview" begins October 1st

Open Enrollment is set at the end of the year to review price increases for the upcoming year. This is the time actually allotted for Medicare users to opt in to Medicare Advantage, Medicare Part C. But, it can be used for other things too. So, even if you're not opting to change to Medicare Part C, you might want to use this time to see if your plan (Medigap or Medicare Advantage) will increase beginning in the upcoming year. During *Open Enrollment*, you could then switch to a more economical plan. Or, let's say during the course of the year, your doctor has prescribed more medications than you used to take. You could take advantage of the Open Enrollment time to determine if a different Medicare Part D prescription plan will offer lower prices for the new meds you now use.

Overall, Open Enrollment is a perfect time to either change from Medigap to Medicare Advantage, to find out if your current Medigap or Medicare Advantage plan will increase in price and find a comparable plan that might be less expensive or to see if a different Medicare Part D plan offers lower prices on the meds you use. This is an ideal time to review your plans and change them if you want.

- Special Enrollment can happen any time; it's Special!
    ◊ It can happen if someone worked past sixty-five, has now retired and wants to enroll in Medicare Part B, Medicare Part D and a Medicare supplement

◊ Or if someone moves to a different area and they want to change plans.

And remember, if you worked past sixty-five, you have eight months from the time your health insurance or employment ends. (Special note: This does not include Cobra) The *Special Enrollment* period can be important for everyone because any time you (or a loved one) move temporarily, or permanently to a skilled nursing facility, this also counts as a 'move,' which oftentimes, is a caveat that is overlooked. You qualify for *Special Election* and you can change your Medicare coverage. If you are making a move to a skilled facility, this is an excellent time to review you supplemental plans and possibly change them. Often, the individual's care has become more critical and a different plan may be more beneficial.

Review your coverage every year. Annual review of your Medicare insurance and review after an acute event cannot be emphasized enough. Many, many seniors who have Medicare just made one decision when they turned sixty-five and they never looked at their plan again, sticking with the same old tried-and-true plan through the years, which can be a costly mistake. If you feel daunted at the prospect of analyzing your Medicare plan again, ask your insurance professional or ask a friend to help you pull up a comparison on their computer as Medicare.gov is a wealth of information to help you make your elections.

Are there any options? The truth is that the bulk of your health care expenses will occur towards the end of your life. Financial experts calculate that Medicare only covers approximately 12 percent of this end-of-life care. Other than just paying out-of-pocket, there are a few options:

- **Supportive Living Facility (SLF)** – If the senior only needs assisted-living, there is the alternative available of a *Supportive Living Facility*. The government pays a portion of the care if the senior meets certain income requirements

- **Long-term care insurance** – Depending on the policy, if a senior has a long-term care insurance policy, they can use its benefits to help defray the cost of home health care, assisted-living and skilled nursing. This will normally pay for a substantial portion of their care

  Long-term care insurance policies have evolved and there are many more 'hybrid' options of long-term care insurance combined with more familiar life insurance products. Also, there are now more embedded safeguards with inflation protection and tax-qualified policies where a portion of the premium is not taxed. In addition, with the newer hybrid plans, if you don't end up needing the long-term care insurance, you do not lose what you've paid into it.

- **Medicaid** -- The senior can go on a "spend down" to qualify for Medicaid (public aid)

Medicaid

You may be thinking there are so many twists, turns and caveats with Medicare and supplemental insurance, that you don't want to deal with; it would be easier to just switch over to Medicaid;

and let the government pay for your health care from this point forward. You may be thinking it would be easy to move your assets over to your kids (and hope they don't spend it all) and then the government will pay for your nursing home expenses. However, the government has covered the bases for situations like these and does a five-year "look back" to see if the senior's assets have been moved.

Plan for the future. Ideally, it's far better for the family to meet with a financial advisor when the senior is younger, healthier and not in a moment of crisis to devise a financial plan for their long-term care. This should also include choosing a durable Power of Attorney for health care and for Finance (Property). It's better—for checks and balances—for two separate people to have these roles. If you're unable to speak for yourself, you need to have someone you trust do this for you (more on this in the *Legal Documents* chapter).

You may be suffering from sticker shock after reading the news about Medicare, but the good news is that Medicare is still statistically much less expensive than the majority of commercial health care insurance plans. The United States is still the envy of the world for the quality and depth of our care. With a little foresight and planning, you can optimize your coverage and plan to make your senior years as sunny and relaxing as possible.

Jean Lyon, MBA, is the owner of Lyon Retirement Solutions, www.lyonretirementsolutions.com, an insurance company dedicated to Medicare insurance. With her extensive background in the senior care and the pharmacy industries, she consults seniors and adult children on their various Medicare choices;

tailoring their needs during Open Enrollment, saving money during annual reviews and assisting with long-term care planning.

For detailed information, please contact Medicare or refer to your Medicare & You 2016 Medicare Handbook. This information is educational in nature regarding senior citizen's health care and Medicare coverage and services. Information contained in this chapter is general in nature, it is not meant to replace the advice of health care professionals. If you have specific health care needs, or for complete information, please see a doctor or other health care provider. Although the author has made every effort to ensure the contents of this information are correct and complete, the author cannot be held responsible for the accuracy of information. Information on Medicare parts and policies may contain inaccuracies, errors or can be changed or updated without notice and therefore may be out of date. This is not a complete listing of plans available in your service area. For a complete listing please contact 1-800-MEDICARE (TTY users should call 1-877-486-2048), 24 hours a day/7 days a week or consult www.medicare.gov.

The Affordable Care Act (ACA)

For many people, there is very little that is affordable about the world Affordable Care Act (ACA) medicine. We get calls every week from people who are frustrated with higher insurance premiums and continuing rising costs of health care. Though it is true that ACA-compliant insurance plans must now cover prevention services at no cost to the consumer, as well as emergency medical services, some customers are frustrated at the rising deductibles that are necessary for affordable insurance premiums. Whether or not all ER visits are covered by insurance is a matter of open debate, as the client usually has out-of-pocket expenses due to higher deductibles necessary for affordable premiums.

Our company does a lot of public service education programs that help educate and empower the public. Education is power. Current information about the rapidly changing health care environment in our country is important for all consumers. As we all age, the chances grow that we will one day be admitted to a hospital at some time. People in crisis do not learn well—anxiety and stress affect how we process information. Therefore, it is best to become knowledgeable about navigating health care challenges before the crisis occurs.

Another challenge for seniors is to find good supplemental plans to their Medicare policies (as discussed in the *Intricacies of Medicare* chapter). Many expensive medications are coming off insurance formularies due to Medicare cost containment. Some of these medicines are critical to those with neurological diseases or undergoing chemotherapy. It is important to have a trusted professional to help weed through the many plans and help consumers choose the right plan for their specific needs. The industry is growing more complex every day and it is hard for the average layperson to know which plan truly is best for their needs. Often, insurance brokers will sell plans that they get the highest sales commissions for. Spending the money today, to hire an advocate who will research your best options, can save you tens of thousands of dollars in the future.

Another group of people affected by modern health care changes are the disabled. This makes me angry because it is the group that needs our country's help the most. Most cannot work and live with serious physical limitations. Unless they are wealthy, they cannot afford the massive costs associated with their disability. The system is set up to control costs and does not always persevere with individuals for the long run. I will expand on this by telling a true story about "William," one of our favorite long-term clients.

William's Story (In the beginning)

William was a 48-year-old engineer living by himself two years ago when he fell off a ladder while changing a light bulb in his kitchen. As he fell, the back of his neck landed sharply on the edge of his kitchen counter—and just like that, William became a quadriplegic. One of his sisters found him and he was transferred to Chicago, to a major health care institution specializing in acute neurological injuries. He received good care initially, but over the course of the following year, he was in and out of 14 hospitals, long-term care facilities, and rehabilitation centers. During that period, William suffered from multiple infections, bed sores, incidents of respiratory failure, and pneumonia. He lost over 35 pounds, developed more infections and was on multiple antibiotics, which eventually resulted in bouts of sepsis from drug-resistant super-infections.

His sisters contacted us last year in desperation. They were afraid he was going to die. They had watched his gradual decline and they knew they had to do something, so they hired a PPHA.

They were frustrated and angry at the insurance company, who kept mandating that he be transferred to low-quality skilled nursing facilities. When we met William, he had a tracheostomy, a feeding gastronomy tube, a catheter, a colostomy, and four large bed sores requiring wound vacuum therapy. He was on a respirator and was covered head-to-toe with severe rashes and flaking skin. His arms and legs were severely contracted and he was in an isolation room for a drug-resistant infection. Though he could not talk, his eyes lit up when he met us and we communicated nonverbally for half an hour. Our presence brought hope to William and his sisters, and they agreed to take a leap of faith in hiring us to advocate in a way that they had been unable to do.

Over the next six weeks, we met regularly with the care manager at his rehab facility to make arrangements for him to come home. The sisters, as well as William himself, knew he would be able to receive the best care at home from people who knew and loved him. As a former ICU nurse, I knew what could be accomplished at home with the right support, and we persevered through many obstacles to get him home. I think the facility staff thought we had all lost our marbles to imagine that we could take such a complex patient home, but his family was determined and we knew we could make it work.

The day came for William to come home and I arrived at his home first to make certain that his equipment had arrived and was functioning properly: much to my dismay, the nursing home care manager had hired a substandard medical supply company and his hospital bed and air mattress were inadequate to ensure that his skin did not break down further. By this point I had developed a working relationship with the insurance company's RN case manager, so I was able to explain all the danger to her and appeal for a much higher-quality bed. Unfortunately, our client ended up back in a local hospital due to wound necrosis. He required surgery to have the wound surgically altered so the healthy tissue could again begin to heal. One thing led to another, and poor practices and sloppy care resulted in multiple complications: pneumonia due to lack of sterile techniques during suctioning; an anemia due to antibiotics that required ten units of blood to be transfused over the next three weeks; and severe anxiety and pain resulting from the adverse medical outcomes that we observed.

Everything was documented and brought to the attention of the hospital staff in a calm, professional manner. Our client's sister was aghast at the lack of infection control measures she observed and was desperate to get her brother out of the hospital. After three weeks, he came home to a brand-new ICU "Cadillac" bed that continually, slowly, rotated him from side to side. The bed had to be specially requested through corporate administration due to the cost: $48,000 retail. It has helped William heal at home, prevent pneumonia occurrences, and also save wear and tear on his family members' backs. They no longer have to wake to turn him every two hours. The bed has been instrumental in keeping him home, healthy, and happy. Twice weekly, skilled nursing visits are paid for by his insurance company and we stay in close contact with his family, helping to avoid needless hospitalizations by intervening early when small problems occur.

When William came back home after his last hospital nightmare, I decided to pay a friendly call to the hospital's risk management department. I politely relayed the things we had observed that were clearly against any hospital's infection control policies. I told them that I had no intention of advising the family to seek legal counsel. But, I said, we also sincerely hoped that this gentleman would receive no bill from the hospital, since three unfortunate instances of medical error had been observed and documented. Our client has never received a bill in the past year since this hospitalization occurred.

Utilization and Management of Health care and Hospital Stays

Not a week goes by that I don't hear stories from seniors, those who care for seniors, and even health care providers who are fed up with the scam of the inpatient vs. observation status controversy. This major rule, which is part of the Affordable Care Act, is costing seniors billions of dollars annually as they get stuck with bills for stays in rehab facilities that are not covered. They were never actually an inpatient in the hospital that treated them and that decided they were too weak to go directly home. The patient is flabbergasted because they thought they were admitted—they slept in the same bed that they would have if they were fully admitted, but they were actually "admitted" under observation status. This cancels their qualification for rehab benefits by Medicare. Emergency room doctors are under heavy pressure to admit every senior they can as an observation patient.

This is a nice way of saying, "We are concerned about you and think you need close watching, so we are going to keep an eye on you to make sure you are well enough to go home." In reality, the patient's bill is higher because many items are not covered under Medicare Part B, which pays for observation or outpatient-type stays. And if the patient goes home after an inpatient admission and returns within 30 days, the hospital is in no hot water from Medicare because they were never technically admitted in the first place. Rehab will only be paid for by Medicare if the patient was a full admission for at least three midnights.

Over and over again we see frail women in their 80s who fall and have a pelvic fracture. If I were an ER physician, I could guess that that elderly woman would be needing rehab post-hospital stay, so I would choose to look carefully for diagnoses and codes that would justify a full admission. That woman probably spent years paying social security; she earned those benefits, right? I'd be thinking of doing the right thing for the patient. A full admission should be justified if she has an actual diagnosis.

But it's not so easy. Hospitals, many of them very good hospitals, are getting huge fines every year if they have too many 30-day readmissions. Medicare sees that as faulty discharge planning, so they will penalize these hospitals with high rates of readmission—with hundreds of thousands of dollars in fines that will ultimately only drive up the cost of American health care. Somebody has to pay for those huge fines, right?

So I am hopping mad about how these policies hurt our seniors and result in frustrated health care workers—who are pushed harder and harder to document more, move along faster than ever, and watch the bottom line above all. From what I can see, business and medicine do not always mix well. Last week I spoke with an emergency room physician who told me, "I knew it was time to stop working in hospitals when they told me I was spending too much time with my patients."

Teri Dreher

You know your own health care spending, but what does the utilization of those dollars look like across the rest of the country? A recent study done by the Dartmouth Institute for Health Policy included a national atlas showing great variations in health care cost and utilization. (Dartmouthatlas.org) Atul Gwande, the physician who wrote the groundbreaking book, 'Being Mortal' in 2014, agrees with many of the conclusions of the Dartmouth study. There is a wide variation in how money on health care is spent in different areas of our country. In population-dense locations where affluence is present, the culture of money encourages physicians and hospitals to order, spend and use more product than in low-income areas. Health care waste and fraud is a big problem in our country, and government restrictions imposed by the Affordable Care Act have done little to rein in costs. Many consumers have noted rising costs of insurance, higher out-of-pocket expenses, and higher hospital bills since 2010 when the ACA was signed into law.

After reviewing the Dartmouth Atlas, several things become apparent to me. First, there is a wide variation in the numbers of seniors who live in different parts of the country. As a general rule, the north and the east coast have a greater percentage of people 75 or older. Generally, fewer seniors want to live in the southwest and Alaska. Second, poverty levels vary greatly in different regions. Older poor people are sicker and utilize greater health care dollars when they do enter the system. It is what it is.

I believe different utilization patterns are also dependent upon how physicians practice in different regions. Studies are showing now that primary care physicians are the best doctors at keeping patients out of hospitals. Most hospitals today use hospitalists to care for inpatients, discouraging primary care physicians from continuing to care for the patients when they enter the institution. Only 50 percent of people nationally have a primary care physician, and often depend upon emergency rooms for acute illnesses. Emergency rooms are the most expensive places of all to receive health care.

Patient culture also factor into utilization. Proximity to hospitals, disease burden, education, race, and economy all play a role as well. It has long been known that older, African-Americans have a general distrust of the American health care system, and often hide their illnesses and refuse to get early intervention for health problems. Diseases such as diabetes and hypertension have a higher prevalence in the African-American community as well, and have serious consequences if left untreated.

Another problem in utilization of health care may be related to Medicare itself. While commercial insurance companies incentivize health care consumers to live healthy lifestyles with lower insurance premiums for quitting smoking, losing weight, and undergoing yearly health assessments, Medicare has no such watchdog programs built in. In fact, slightly over 10 percent of Medicare recipients nationally take advantage of yearly free health checkups with their doctors.

Tips to Equip: Navigating the choppy Medicare waters

- Verify your admission status (Obs ensures you will receive higher bills than inpt) before being transferring to a rehab facility to prevent the sticker shock of a surprise bill by the rehab facility

- You must sign up for Medicare, it is **not** automatic when you age to 65

- You must sign up for Medicare, on time, or risk permanent increased premiums for Medicare due to late enrollment fees

- An insurance professional with Medicare expertise is an excellent option to help avail you of the many options you have to suit your needs

- Please visit Medicare.gov to help you become informed of your options for supplemental insurance as well as other Medicare-related information

- The bottom line is, your Medicare card only covers the Medicare Part A premium. You must pay for the premium for Medicare Part B, Medicare Part D and your Medicare supplement insurance. If you need long-term care, most of that is private pay

- A PPHA can help research and provide you with your best options in addition to saving you money in the future

Chapter 11

Legal Documents

Legal documents

No one likes to talk about them, but every one needs them. It is one of the most difficult, but vitally necessary legal forms that all adults should have – a health care power of attorney. A health care power of attorney names a surrogate decision-maker who can step in and make health care decisions on a person's behalf. It is a more legal and binding document than a living will, and it is the one that hospitals always ask for when a person arrives at the hospital unconscious. A person must be mentally competent to assign another person rights to act as a health care power of attorney. If the senior becomes mentally incompetent, or unable to make their own decisions due to a stroke, dementia, or any condition that renders them unconscious, the family will need to go to court to have a legal guardian assigned. This can be costly and time-consuming.

In the short term, hospitals may ask the family to assign a family member "surrogate decision-maker" status, but for long-term decisions, a guardianship procedure will be necessary for patients who do not have a health care power of attorney documented. The form can be easily obtained on each state government's website and usually does not need to be notarized. Families can do the documentation themselves, but it is wise to have a health care professional or attorney assist them, in case the issue of competence should be questioned by anyone at a later time. Financial/household power-of-attorney designation should always be done with an attorney present, as is true with wills and trusts. If a person dies without a will or trust, the person's estate will be dispersed by the probate court. Going through probate is time-consuming and expensive, as the court takes a percentage of the estate's value for court costs. Planning ahead will avoid frustration and save time and money for all concerned.

There are other ethical dilemmas out there in the new world of health care that concern me. One controversial law, which has been adopted in many states, is called the POLST (Physician Order for Life-Sustaining Treatment). It replaces the old Do Not Resuscitate order that families and physicians would sign when they determined that heroic measures would no longer be used if the patient stopped breathing or had a cardiac arrest. The POLST law adds some new caveats that some people feel give physicians too much control in life-or-death situations. I learned this in the case of a young woman I will call Wu-Lin.

Wu-Lin's Story

Wu-Lin and her husband were both doctoral students at a large university on the near North Side of Chicago. They were delighted when Wu-Lin became pregnant with their first child, a son. This would be the first grandson on both sides of the family, and their parents and Wu-Lin's brother were all in China awaiting the happy event.

One morning, Wu-Lin woke up with a severe headache. It progressed and caused sensitivity to light, nausea, and vomiting. Her husband rushed her to the local emergency room, where the doctors saw signs that indicated an intra-cranial bleed, so they ordered a stat MRI scam. While Wu-Lin was in the MRI room, she started seizing and a code blue was called. She had developed an intra-cranial hemorrhage from a small aneurysm, stressed by the increased circulating blood volume of pregnancy. She was 28 years old and eight months pregnant.

Physicians rushed to MRI and put her on life support, performed a crash C-section (saving the baby boy), inserted an intraventricular drain in her skull to relieve the pressure and evacuate the blood, and sent her to ICU. When frantic family members contacted me two days later, it was because doctors were telling, not asking, the family that life support would be removed the following day.

When I walked into her room in the ICU that afternoon, I could see signs of brain death: fixed, dilated pupils; copious amounts of urine draining from her catheter (diabetes insipidus occurs when the mid-brain is damaged and the body loses its ability to regulate fluids properly); high doses of three vasopressors; a very fast hart rate; a very low blood pressure. After confirming the doctor's report that she appeared to be brain-dead, I spent time with the family, listening to the devastation they were going through.

The mother of this beautiful young woman was concerned about getting her son to the US before she died; the doctors were pushing hard to have Wu-Lin's life support removed before her brother could get his emergency visa and come to Chicago-O'Hare the following day. In the Dhao religion, if a person dies on the wrong day of the Chinese calendar, they will not be reunited with their ancestors. This was important to the family; Wu-Lin should die on a good day.

That evening, we convened with the family at a patient care conference. Wu-Lin's grieving family and the doctors assigned to her case met for several hours to try and reach a resolution. The doctors told them that since she had been declared brain-dead, they did not need permission to remove her life support. And technically, they were right. The POLST law makes it clear that once someone has been declared brain-dead, they are legally dead.

I had never personally seen doctors use that prerogative in a case such as this. The neurosurgeon on Wu-Lin's case was particularly abrasive and insensitive to the grieving family. At one point, the mother of the dying woman threw herself down upon the carpet, sobbing hysterically.

I *stopped the meeting and requested a full ethics committee meeting to evaluate the case the following day.*

Hospitals don't like it when outsiders request an ethics committee hearing. It means that community members who sit on the committee will hear the hospital's dirty laundry aired publicly. It means that someone on the outside questions the ethics and integrity of the hospital. It's embarrassing.

The following day, around two dozen of us crowded into a hospital conference room to hear from the family. Through a Mandarin interpreter, they told a poignant story of who Wu-Lin was: a brilliant scholar, a beautiful young woman filled with hope, someone with a bright future. She was a loving wife, a kind and tender mother-to-be.

The family told a much more difficult story as well: one of cold, stern, and uncompromising physicians who betrayed no sensitivity for what the family was going through. I looked around the room as ethics committee members grew shocked and sad. When the doctors were mentioned, people looked down at their hands or turned away, sometimes with tears in their eyes. Wu-Lin's husband looked into my eyes the entire time he spoke, and told me afterward that my face gave him courage to go on. He and his mother-in-law embraced me, thanking me for standing by them and giving them courage as they spoke.

I will probably never know why the doctors were so insistent on being the ones to determine the hour of Wu-Lin's death. The ICU had six empty beds that day, so I cannot imagine what the rush was. The ethics committee suggested that they allow the family the extra time they requested for Wu-Lin's brother to arrive. Instead, the doctors removed her life support one hour before his plane landed the following day.

I don't know if money played a role in this case or not, but I do know that hospitals are under pressure these days to contain costs and justify utilization of health care dollars. Who knows? It may have simply been a control issue.

Wu-Lin's husband ultimately went back to China with his parents and in-laws. They are helping him raise his son, whose name means "happy" in Mandarin.

Tips to Equip: Getting your documents in order

- Assign a health care power of attorney to make health care decisions for you, should you become incapacitated

- Separately, if possible, assign a financial designation and should be done with an attorney present

- If you die without a will, your estate could be held up for years in probate court. Not only will this be costly and time consuming for the loved ones you've left behind, the court takes a piece of your estate in addition to deciding how it will be dispersed between your family

- Check into your state's laws regarding Do Not Resuscitate orders; they may have changed to empower physicians to enact the new POLST order. This gives physicians more power than your family to decide when you legally 'die'

It All Comes Down To This

So, by now, you've come to realize just how crucial the task of advocating for yourself or your loved one is to the quality of your life, your health and your rights. This book is your invitation and toolkit to patients and families everywhere to become an active participant and an informed healthcare consumer who will not settle for anything less than safe, high-quality medical care.

My colleagues and I have covered the gamut from what it means to be an advocate, all of the different considerations at stake, such as legal documents; alternate means of treatment; your rights under various circumstances as well as how to exert them. I covered how to protect yourself in different situations; whether that is your person, your safety or your belongings, as well as who can benefit from having an advocate, which is the easiest question to answer of them all: any one who is a health care recipient can benefit from having an advocate on their side.

I've covered what it takes to be an advocate as well as the different types of advocates available; and which type of advocate has the most resources at their disposal to solve a complex set of problems as an advocate, which I firmly believe will always be the nurse advocate. Simply put, it is because of our far-reaching background, which spans the plethora of specialties, situations and challenges we've faced as nurses throughout our respective, clinical careers.

I will reiterate the fact that there are many types of advocates, so hopefully, I've provided enough information and tips to equip, educate and empower you to help you do your due diligence in choosing the one that will protect your interests best, if you decide an advocate is the right way to go for your unique situation.

I would be remiss to end this extensive collection of valuable tips and information without summarizing how effective a champion nurse advocates can be, least of all for the "perks" we provide, one of which is simply being there to help health care recipients digest, and effectively utilize, the plethora of information they receive, especially in this new world of modern health care.

Depending on the situation, a nurse advocate, who is medically trained, can also put together a complete medical profile for you that is worth its weight in gold. This can be especially helpful if you're seeing multiple physicians, or you make unscheduled trips to the ER, as a way to improve communication between physicians-especially where your health is concerned. Depending on how savvy you are, the complete medical profile may cover the extent of what you may need to carry forward on your own, or with very little other supporting assistance needed from a nurse advocate on a regular basis.

The big takeaway I have endeavored to leave you with is my, and many of my colleagues', concern for patients in this ever-changing world of health care, and the ability to navigate it successfully, and have positive outcomes. In other words, to be quite frank, I am very concerned for the safety of health care recipients in this current era of modern health care.

Even though nurses and physicians are doing the very best they can, to give high-quality, safe and efficient care with the increased demands in the post Affordable Care Act world, we also know, in a way that only we can, as clinicians, how the system can fail patients.

My hope for this book is that it will reach–and ultimately–help, in some way–on a global scale, more health care recipients than I can ever hope to reach, patient-to-patient, since it is literally impossible to save every, single person who could benefit from the many resources at my disposal.

While I know it is likely to take a long time to fix our broken health care system, we, as patients and the loved ones of patients, need to advocate for ourselves, or get someone who knows how to advocate for us. A private professional health care advocate is someone you should ideally have on speed dial at all times, but barring that, I pray this book may serve a multitude of patients that may not be able to hire one.

References

American Hospital Association. https://www.aha.org.

Alliance of Professional Health Advocates. (2016). About APHA. Retrieved June 20, 2016, from aphaadvocates. org: www.aphaadvocates.org/about-apha/

Alzheimer's Association. (n.d.). 2015 Alzheimer's Disease Facts and Figures. Retrieved from alz.org: https://www.alz.org/ facts/downloads/facts_figures_2015.pdfhttps://www.alz.org/ facts/downloads/facts_figures_2015.pdf

Alzheimers Association. (2016). Residential Care. Retrieved July 8, 2016, from alz.org: http://www.alz.org/care/ alzheimers-dementia-residential-facilities.asp#types

American Geriatric Society. (n.d.). Identifying Medications that Older Adults Should Avoid or Use With Caution: the 2012 American Geriatrics Society Updated Beers Criteria. Retrieved from americangeriatrics.org: http:// www.americangeriatrics.org/files/documents/beers/ BeersCriteriaPublicTranslation.pdf

American Hospital Association. (n.d.). Patient Care Partnership. Retrieved from aha.org: www.aha.org/content/00-10/pcp_ english_030730.pdf

Andrews, L. B., Stocking, C., & Krizek, T. (1997). An Alternative Method for Studying Adverse Events in Medical Care. Lancet , 349, 309-313.

Teri Dreher

Beckers Hospital Review. (2016). 10 Top Patient Safety Issues
For 2016. Retrieved from www.beckershospitalreview.com:
http://www.beckershospitalreview.com/quality/10-top-patient-
safety-issues-for-2016.htmlhttp://www.beckershospitalreview.
com/quality/10-top-patient-safety-issues-for-2016.html

Bureau of Labor Statistics. (2015, May). 29-1126 Respiratory
Therapist. Retrieved June 27, 2016, from bls.gov:
http://www.bls.gov/oes/current/oes291126.htm

Cancer Centers Of America. https://www.cancercenter.com

Centers for Disease Control and Prevention. (n.d.). Hand Hygiene.
Retrieved June 21, 2016, from www.cdc.gov: https://www.cdc.
gov/HandHygiene/download/hand_hygiene_core.pdf

Centers for Disease Control and Prevention. (2016, April 28).
Hand Hygiene in Healthcare Settings. Retrieved May 27,
2016, from www.cdc.gov.

Centers for Disease Control and Prevention. (2016, March 3).
Making Health Care Safer. Retrieved June 1, 2016, from
www.cdc.gov: www.cdc.gov/vitalsigns/protect-patients/

Centers for Disease Control. (2016, March 31). cdc.gov.
Retrieved April 20, 2016, from Autism Spectrum Disorder:
http://www.cdc.gov/ncbddd/autism/data.html

Dartmouth Atlas. http://www.Dartmouthatlas.org

Gallup. (2014, December 18). Americans Rate Nurses Highest
on Honesty, Ethical Standards. Retrieved June 11, 2016, from
gallup.com: http://www.gallup.com/poll/180260/americans-
rate-nurses-highest-honesty-ethical-standards.aspx

Institute for Safe Medicine Practices. (2015). ISMP's list of confused drug names. Retrieved June 12, 2016, from ismp. org: http://www.ismp.org/Tools/confuseddrugnames.pdf

Japsen, B. (2016, March 6). Retrieved May 27, 2016, from www.forbes.com: http://www.forbes.com/sites/ brucejapsen/2016/03/06/states-remove-barriers-to-physician- assistants/#60b5583314e7

Jauhar, S. (2014, August 29). Why Doctors Are Sick Of Their Profession. Retrieved June 4, 2016, from www.wsj.com: http://www.wsj.com/articles/the-u-s-s-ailing-medical-system- a-doctors-perspective-1409325361

John T. James, P. (2014). A New, Evidence-Based Estimate Of Patient Harms Associated With Hospital Care. Journal of Patient Safety , 9 (3), 122-128.

Linda T. Kohn, J. M. (2000). To err is human: building a safer health system. National Academy of Sciences. Washington DC: National Academy Press.

Medicare. (n.d.). Skilled Nursing Facility Checklist. Retrieved from medicare.gov: https://www.medicare.gov/files/skilled- nursing-facility-checklist.pdf

Met Life Market Institute. (2011). Market Survey of Long-Term Care Costs: The 2011 MetLife Market Survey of Nursing Home, Assisted Living, Adult Day Services, and Home Care Costs. New York: Metropolitan Life Insurance Company.

NAHAC. (2015). History of NAHAC. Retrieved June 25, 2016, from www.nahac.memberlodge.com: www.nahac. memberlodge.com/history

NAHAC. (2015). www.nahac.memberlodge.com. Retrieved June 25, 2016, from http://nahac.memberlodge.com

National Association of Orthopedic Technologists. (2013). What is an orthopedic technologist? Retrieved July 1, 2016, from naot.org: http://www.naot.org/sections/about.orthotics.php

Patient Advocate Certification Board. (n.d.). Patient Advocacy vs. Medical Advocacy: View from the PACB. Retrieved from pacboard.org: http://pacboard.org/2016/03/09/patient-advocacy-vs-medical-advocacy-view-from-the-pacb/

Pew Research Center. (2013). The Sandwich Generation. Retrieved March 20, 2016, from pewsocialtrends.org: http://www.pewsocialtrends.org/2013/01/30/the-sandwich-generation/

Index

A

C

D

E

F

H

I

L

M

N

O

Obama Care, 29, 30, 157
observation, 34, 35, 78, 94, 97, 161, 162, 164, 178
Over-The-Counter, 143

P

palliative care, 72, 73
Patient advocacy, 14
Patient Bill of Rights, 7, 63, 65, 66, 91, 116
Physician Order for Life-Sustaining Treatment, 183
physiology, 147, 148, 155
Polypharmacy, 118
positive outcome. See successful outcomes, See successful outcomes
power of attorney, 67, 79, 85, 126, 128, 183, 187
PPHA, 7, 53, 62, 63, 80, 108, 111, 131, 162, 176, 181
prescriptions. See medications, See medications, See medications, See medications
primary care physician, 25, 87, 113, 180
primary care physicians, 28, 33, 34, 68, 179
Privacy of health information, 92
private insurance, 29, 32, 53, 167
Private Professional Health Advocate, 44
proper protocol, 103
psychology of illness, 146

Q

R

S

T

U

V

W

CPSIA information can be obtained
at www.ICGtesting.com
Printed in the USA
LVOW10s1259240717
542431LV00022B/694/P